797,885 Books

are available to read at

www.ForgottenBooks.com

---◆---

Forgotten Books' App
Available for mobile, tablet & eReader

ISBN 978-1-330-71922-0
PIBN 10096582

This book is a reproduction of an important historical work. Forgotten Books uses state-of-the-art technology to digitally reconstruct the work, preserving the original format whilst repairing imperfections present in the aged copy. In rare cases, an imperfection in the original, such as a blemish or missing page, may be replicated in our edition. We do, however, repair the vast majority of imperfections successfully; any imperfections that remain are intentionally left to preserve the state of such historical works.

1 MONTH OF
FREE
READING

at
www.ForgottenBooks.com

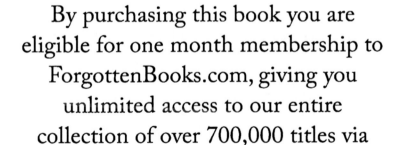

By purchasing this book you are
eligible for one month membership to
ForgottenBooks.com, giving you
unlimited access to our entire
collection of over 700,000 titles via
our web site and mobile apps.

To claim your free month visit:
www.forgottenbooks.com/free96582

Similar Books Are Available from
www.forgottenbooks.com

¶ Of this edition of the SELECTED POEMS OF THOMAS HARDY have been printed in the Riccardi fount on hand-made Riccardi Paper 1025 copies, of which 1000 only are for sale, and upon Vellum 14 copies, of which 12 are for sale.

¶ Paper copy Number   265

SELECTED POEMS
OF THOMAS HARDY

SELECTED POEMS OF THOMAS HARDY WITH PORTRAIT & TITLE PAGE DESIGN ENGRAVED ON THE WOOD BY WILLIAM NICHOLSON

PHILIP LEE WARNER, PUBLISHER TO THE MEDICI SOCIETY LTD., LONDON, LIVERPOOL AND BOSTON. MDCCCCXXI

First published in The Golden
Treasury Series 1916. Reprinted
in the Riccardi Press Books 1921

CONTENTS
PART I
POEMS CHIEFLY LYRICAL

PART II

POEMS NARRATIVE AND REFLECTIVE

PART III

WAR POEMS AND LYRICS FROM 'THE DYNASTS'

PART ONE: POEMS CHIEFLY LYRICAL

b

AFTER THE VISIT

To F. E. D.

COME again to the place
  Where your presence was as a leaf that skims
Down a drouthy way whose ascent bedims
    The bloom on the farer's face.

  Come again, with the feet
That were light on the green as a thistledown ball,
And those mute ministrations to one and to all
    Beyond a man's saying sweet.

  Until then the faint scent
Of the bordering flowers swam unheeded away,
And I marked not the charm in the changes of day
    As the cloud-colours came and went.

  Through the dark corridors
Your walk was so soundless I did not know
Your form from a phantom's of long ago
    Said to pass on the ancient floors,

  Till you drew from the shade,
And I saw the large luminous living eyes
Regard me in fixed inquiring-wise
    As those of a soul that weighed,

  Scarce consciously,
The eternal question of what Life was,
And why we were there, and by whose strange laws
    That which mattered most could not be.

TO MEET, OR OTHERWISE

WHETHER to sally and see thee, girl of my
  dreams,
  Or whether to stay
And see thee not! How vast the difference seems
  Of Yea from Nay
Just now. Yet this same sun will slant its beams
  At no far day
On our two mounds, & then what will the difference
  weigh!

  Yet I will see thee, maiden dear, and make
    The most I can
  Of what remains to us amid this brake
    Cimmerian
  Through which we grope, and from whose thorns
    we ache,
    While still we scan
Round our frail faltering progress for some path or
    plan.

  By briefest meeting something sure is won;
    It will have been:
  Nor God nor Demon can undo the done,
    Unsight the seen,
  Make muted music be as unbegun,
    Though things terrene
Groan in their bondage till oblivion supervene.

  So, to the one long-sweeping symphony
    From times remote

Till now, of human tenderness, shall we
    Supply one note,
Small and untraced, yet that will ever be
    Somewhere afloat
Amid the spheres, as part of sick Life's antidote.

THE DIFFERENCE

I

SINKING down by the gate I discern the thin
    moon,
And a blackbird tries over old airs in the pine,
But the moon is a sorry one, sad the bird's tune,
For this spot is unknown to that Heartmate of mine.

II

Did my Heartmate but haunt here at times such as
    now,
The song would be joyous and cheerful the moon;
But she will see never this gate, path, or bough,
Nor I find a joy in the scene or the tune.

ON THE DEPARTURE PLATFORM

WE kissed at the barrier; and passing through
    She left me, and moment by moment got
Smaller and smaller, until to my view
    She was but a spot;

A wee white spot of muslin fluff
That down the diminishing platform bore
Through hustling crowds of gentle and rough
    To the carriage door.

Under the lamplight's fitful glowers,
Behind dark groups from far and near
Whose interests were apart from ours,
   She would disappear,

Then show again, till I ceased to see
That flexible form, that nebulous white;
And she who was more than my life to me
   Had vanished quite

We have penned new plans since that fair fond day,
And in season she will appear again –
Perhaps in the same soft white array –
   But never as then!

'And why, young man, must eternally fly
A joy you'll repeat, if you love her well?'
  O friend, nought happens twice thus; why,
   I cannot tell!

IN A CATHEDRAL CITY

THESE people have not heard your name;
  No loungers in this placid place
Have helped to bruit your beauty's fame.

  The grey Cathedral, towards whose face
  Bend eyes untold, has met not yours;
  Your shade has never swept its base,

  Your form has never darked its doors,
  Nor have your faultless feet once thrown
  A pensive pit-pat on its floors.

Along the street to maidens known
Blithe lovers hum their tender airs,
But in your praise voice not a tone.

~Since nought bespeaks you here, or bears,
As I, your imprint through and through,
Here might I rest, till my heart shares
The spot's unconsciousness of you!

Salisbury

'I SAY I'LL SEEK HER'

I SAY, 'I'll seek her side
Ere hindrance interposes';
   But eve in midnight closes,
And here I still abide.

When darkness wears I see
   Her sad eyes in a vision;
   They ask, 'What indecision
Detains you, Love, from me?

'The creaking hinge is oiled,
   I have unbarred the backway,
   But you tread not the trackway;
And shall the thing be spoiled?

'Far cockcrows echo shrill,
   The shadows are abating,
   And I am waiting, waiting;
But O, you tarry still!'

SONG OF HOPE

O SWEET To-morrow!
    After to-day
    There will away
This sense of sorrow.
Then let us borrow
Hope, for a gleaming
Soon will be streaming,
    Dimmed by no gray
        No gray!

While the winds wing us
    Sighs from The Gone,
    Nearer to dawn
Minute-beats bring us;
When there will sing us
Larks, of a glory
Waiting our story
    Further anon –
        Anon!

Doff the black token,
    Don the red shoon,
    Right and retune
Viol-strings broken;
Null the words spoken
In speeches of rueing,
The night cloud is hueing,
    To-morrow shines soon
        Shines soon!

BEFORE AND AFTER SUMMER

I

LOOKING forward to the spring
One puts up with anything.
On this February day,
Though the winds leap down the street
Wintry scourgings seem but play,
And these later shafts of sleet
- Sharper pointed than the first -
And these later snows - the worst -
Are as a half-transparent blind
Riddled by rays from sun behind.

II

Shadows of the October pine
Reach into this room of mine:
On the pine there swings a bird;
He is shadowed with the tree.
Mutely perched he bills no word;
Blank as I am even is he.
For those happy suns are past,
Fore-discerned in winter last.
When went by their pleasure, then?
I, alas, perceived not when.

FIRST SIGHT OF HER AND AFTER

A DAY is drawing to its fall
I had not dreamed to see;
The first of many to enthrall
My spirit, will it be?

Or is this eve the end of all
    Such new delight for me?

I journey home: the pattern grows
    Of moon-shades on the way:
'Soon the first quarter, I suppose,'
    Sky-glancing travellers say.
I realize that it, for those,
    Has been a common day.

THE SUN ON THE BOOKCASE

Student's Love-song

ONCE more the cauldron of the sun
    Smears the bookcase with winy red,
And here my page is, and there my bed,
And the apple-tree shadows travel along.
Soon their intangible track will be run,
    And dusk grow strong
    And they have fled.

Yes: now the boiling ball is gone.
And I have wasted another day.
But wasted~w a s t e d, do I say?
Is it a waste to have imaged one
Beyond the hills there, who, anon,
    My great deeds done,
    Will be mine alway?
1870

'WHEN I SET OUT FOR LYONNESSE'

WHEN I set out for Lyonnesse,
    A hundred miles away,
    The rime was on the spray,

And starlight lit my lonesomeness
When I set out for Lyonnesse
A hundred miles away.

What would bechance at Lyonnesse
While I should sojourn there
No prophet durst declare,
Nor did the wisest wizard guess
What would bechance at Lyonnesse
While I should sojourn there.

When I came back from Lyonnesse
With magic in my eyes,
All marked with mute surmise
My radiance rare and fathomless,
When I came back from Lyonnesse
With magic in my eyes!

1870

AT THE WORD 'FAREWELL'

SHE looked like a bird from a cloud
On the clammy lawn,
Moving alone, bare-browed,
In the dim of dawn.
The candles alight in the room
For my parting meal
Made all things withoutdoors loom
Strange, ghostly, unreal.

The hour itself was a ghost,
And it seemed to me then
As of chances the chance furthermost
I should see her again.

I beheld not where all was so fleet
    That a Plan of the past
Which had ruled us from birthtime to meet
    Was accomplished at last.

No prelude did I there perceive
    To a drama at all,
Or foreshadow what fortune might weave
    From beginnings so small.
But I rose as if quicked by a spur
    I was bound to obey,
And stepped through the casement to her
    Still alone in the gray.

'I am leaving you.   Farewell!' I said
    As I followed her on
By an alley bare boughs overspread:
    'I soon must be gone!'
Even then the scale might have been turned
    Against love by a feather,
  But crimson one cheek of hers burned
    When we came in together.

DITTY

E. L. G.

BENEATH a knap where flown
    Nestlings play,
Within walls of weathered stone,
    Far away
From the files of formal houses,
By the bough the firstling browses,
Lives a Sweet: no merchants meet,
No man barters, no man sells
    Where she dwells.

Upon that fabric fair
  'Here is she!'
Seems written everywhere
  Unto me.
But to friends and nodding neighbours,
Fellow-wights in lot and labours,
Who descry the times as I,
No such lucid legend tells
  Where she dwells.

Should I lapse to what I was
  Ere we met;
(Such will not be, but because
  Some forget
Let me feign it)–none would notice
That where she I know by rote is
Spread a strange and withering change,
Like a drying of the wells
  Where she dwells.

To feel I might have kissed–
  Loved as true–
Otherwhere, nor Mine have missed
  My life through,
Had I never wandered near her,
Is a smart severe–severer
In the thought that she is nought,
Even as I, beyond the dells
  Where she dwells.

And Devotion droops her glance
  To recall

What bondservants of Chance
    We are all.
I but found her in that, going
On my errant path unknowing,
I did not out-skirt the spot
That no spot on earth excels,
    ~Where she dwells!
1870

THE NIGHT OF THE DANCE

THE cold moon hangs to the sky by its horn,
    And centres its gaze on me;
The stars, like eyes in reverie,
Their westering as for a while forborne,
    Quiz downward curiously.

Old Robert hauls the backbrand in,
    The green logs steam and spit;
The half-awakened sparrows flit
From the riddled thatch; and owls begin
    To whoo from the gable-slit.

Yes; far and nigh things seem to know
    Sweet scenes are impending here;
That all is prepared; that the hour is near
For welcomes, fellowships, and flow
    Of sally, song, and cheer;

That spigots are pulled and viols strung;
    That soon will arise the sound
Of measures trod to tunes renowned;
That She will return in Love's low tongue
    My vows as we wheel around.

O LIZBIE BROWNE

I

DEAR Lizbie Browne,
Where are you now?
In sun, in rain? –
Or is your brow
Past joy, past pain,
Dear Lizbie Browne?

II

Sweet Lizbie Browne,
How you could smile,
How you could sing!
How archly wile
In glance-giving,
Sweet Lizbie Browne!

III

And, Lizbie Browne,
Who else had hair
Bay-red as yours,
Or flesh so fair
Bred out of doors,
Sweet Lizbie Browne?

IV

When, Lizbie Browne,
You had just begun
To be endeared
By stealth to one,
You disappeared
My Lizbie Browne!

V

Ay, Lizbie Browne,
So swift your life,
And mine so slow,
You were a wife
Ere I could show
Love, Lizbie Browne.

VI

Still, Lizbie Browne,
You won, they said,
The best of men
When you were wed.
Where went you then,
O Lizbie Browne?

VII

Dear Lizbie Browne,
I should have thought,
'Girls ripen fast,'
And coaxed and caught
You ere you passed,
Dear Lizbie Browne!

VIII

But, Lizbie Browne,
I let you slip;
Shaped not a sign;
Touched never your lip
With lip of mine,
Lost Lizbie Browne!

IX

So, Lizbie Browne,
When on a day
Men speak of me
As not, you'll say,
'And who was he?'—
Yes, Lizbie Browne!

'LET ME ENJOY'

I

LET me enjoy the earth no less
  Because the all-enacting Might
That fashioned forth its loveliness
Had other aims than my delight.

II

About my path there flits a Fair,
Who throws me not a word or sign;
I'll charm me with her ignoring air,
And laud the lips not meant for mine.

III

From manuscripts of moving song
Inspired by scenes and dreams unknown
I'll pour out raptures that belong
To others, as they were my own.

IV

And some day hence, toward Paradise
And all its blest—if such should be
I will lift glad, afar-off eyes,
Though it contain no place for me.

THE BALLAD-SINGER

SING, Ballad-singer, raise a hearty tune;
  Make me forget that there was ever a one
I walked with in the meek light of the moon
    When the day's work was done.

Rhyme, Ballad-rhymer, start a country song;
Make me forget that she whom I loved well
Swore she would love me dearly, love me long,
    Then-what I cannot tell!

Sing, Ballad-singer, from your little book;
Make me forget those heart-breaks, achings, fears;
Make me forget her name, her sweet, sweet look
    Make me forget her tears.

THE DIVISION

RAIN on the windows, creaking doors,
  With blasts that besom the green,
    And I am here, and you are there,
      And a hundred miles between!

    O were it but the weather, Dear,
      O were it but the miles
    That summed up all our severance,
      There might be room for smiles.

    But that thwart thing betwixt us twain,
      Which nothing cleaves or clears,
    Is more than distance, Dear, or rain,
      And longer than the years!

189-

YELL'HAM-WOOD'S STORY

COOMB-FIRTREES say that Life is a moan,
And Clyffe-hill Clump says 'Yea!'
But Yell'ham says a thing of its own:
    It's not 'Gray, gray
    Is Life alway!'
    That Yell'ham says,
Nor that Life is for ends unknown.

It says that Life would signify
    A thwarted purposing:
That we come to live, and are called to die.
    Yes, that's the thing
    In fall, in spring,
    That Yell'ham says·
'Life offers - to deny!'

1902

HER INITIALS

UPON a poet's page I wrote
    Of old two letters of her name;
Part seemed she of the effulgent thought
Whence that high singer's rapture came.

- When now I turn the leaf the same
Immortal light illumes the lay,
But from the letters of her name
The radiance has waned away!

1869

19

THE WOUND

I CLIMBED to the crest,
  And, fog-festooned,
The sun lay west
Like a crimson wound:

Like that wound of mine
Of which none knew,
For I'd given no sign
That it pierced me through.

A MERRYMAKING IN QUESTION

'I WILL get a new string for my fiddle,
  And call to the neighbours to come,
And partners shall dance down the middle
    Until the old pewter-wares hum;
And we'll sip the mead, cyder, and rum!'

From the night came the oddest of answers:
    A hollow wind, like a bassoon,
And headstones all ranged up as dancers,
    And cypresses droning a croon,
And gurgoyles that mouthed to the tune.

'HOW GREAT MY GRIEF'

Triolet

HOW great my grief, my joys how few,
  Since first it was my fate to know thee!
~ Have the slow years not brought to view
How great my grief, my joys how few,

Nor memory shaped old times anew,
    Nor loving-kindness helped to show thee
How great my grief, my joys how few,
    Since first it was my fate to know thee?

AT AN INN

WHEN we as strangers sought
    Their catering care,
Veiled smiles bespoke their thought
    Of what we were.
They warmed as they opined
    Us more than friends
That we had all resigned
    For love's dear ends.

And that swift sympathy
    With living love
Which quicks the world – maybe
    The spheres above,
Made them our ministers,
    Moved them to say,
'Ah, God, that bliss like theirs
    Would flush our day!'

And we were left alone
    As Love's own pair;
Yet never the love-light shone
    Between us there,
But that which chilled the breath
    Of afternoon,
And palsied unto death
    The pane-fly's tune.

The kiss their zeal foretold,
    And now deemed come,
Came not: within his hold
    Love lingered numb.
Why cast he on our port
    A bloom not ours?
Why shaped us for his sport
    In after-hours?

As we seemed we were not
    That day afar,
And now we seem not what
    We aching are.
O severing sea and land,
    O laws of men,
Ere death, once let us stand
    As we stood then!

A BROKEN APPOINTMENT

YOU did not come,
    And marching Time drew on and wore me
    numb.
Yet less for loss of your dear presence there
Than that I thus found lacking in your make
That high compassion which can overbear
Reluctance for pure loving-kindness' sake
Grieved I, when, as the hope-hour stroked its sum,
        You did not come.

        You love not me,
And love alone can lend you loyalty;
–I know and knew it. But, unto the store

Of human deeds divine in all but name,
Was it not worth a little hour or more
To add yet this: Once, you, a woman, came
To soothe a time-torn man; even though it be
    You love not me?

AT NEWS OF A WOMAN'S DEATH

NOT a line of her writing have I,
    Not a thread of her hair,
No mark of her late time as dame in her dwelling,
        whereby
    I may picture her there;
    And in vain do I urge my unsight
        To conceive my lost prize
At her close, whom I knew when her dreams were
        upbrimming with light,
    And with laughter her eyes.

    What scenes spread around her last days,
        Sad, shining, or dim?
Did her gifts and compassions enray and enarch her
        sweet ways
    With an aureate nimb?
    Or did life-light decline from her years,
        And mischances control
Her full day-star; unease, or regret, or forebodings,
        or fears
    Disennoble her soul?

    Thus I do but the phantom retain
        Of the maiden of yore

As my relic; yet haply the best of her—fined in my
      brain
    It may be the more
  That no line of her writing have I,
    Nor a thread of her hair,
No mark of her late time as dame in her dwelling,
      whereby
    I may picture her there.

March 1890

MIDDLE-AGE ENTHUSIASMS

To M. H.

WE passed where flag and flower
    Signalled a jocund throng;
We said: 'Go to, the hour
Is apt!'—and joined the song;
And, kindling, laughed at life and care,
Although we knew no laugh lay there.

  We walked where shy birds stood
  Watching us, wonder-dumb;
  Their friendship met our mood;
  We cried: 'We'll often come:
We'll come morn, noon, eve, everywhen!'
  We doubted we should come again.

  We joyed to see strange sheens
  Leap from quaint leaves in shade;
  A secret light of greens
  They'd for their pleasure made.
We said: 'We'll set such sorts as these!'
—We knew with night the wish would cease.

24

'So sweet the place,' we said,
'Its tacit tales so dear,
Our thoughts, when breath has sped,
Will meet and mingle here!' . . .
'Words!' mused we. 'Passed the mortal door,
Our thoughts will reach this nook no more.'

IN A EWELEAZE

THE years have gathered grayly
　　Since I danced upon this leaze
With one who kindled gaily
　　Love's fitful ecstasies!
But despite the term as teacher
　　I remain what I was then
In each essential feature
　　Of the fantasies of men.

Yet I note the little chisel
　　Of never-napping Time
Defacing ghast and grizzel
　　The blazon of my prime.
When at night he thinks me sleeping
　　I feel him boring sly
Within my bones, and heaping
　　Quaintest pains for by and by.

Still, I'd go the world with Beauty,
　　I would laugh with her and sing,
I would shun divinest duty
　　To resume her worshipping.

e

But she'd scorn my brave endeavour,
  She would not balm the breeze
By murmuring 'Thine for ever!'
  As she did upon this leaze.

1890

A SPOT

IN years defaced and lost,
  Two sat here, transport-tossed,
  Lit by a living love
The wilted world knew nothing of:
      Scared momently
      By gaingivings,
      Then hoping things
      That could not be.

  Of love and us no trace
  Abides upon the place;
  The sun and shadows wheel,
Season and season sere-ward steal;
      Foul days and fair
      Here, too, prevail,
      And gust and gale
      As everywhere.

  But lonely shepherd souls
  Who bask amid these knolls
  May catch a faery sound
On sleepy noontides from the ground:
      'O not again
      Till Earth outwears
      Shall love like theirs
      Suffuse this glen!'

THE DARKLING THRUSH

I LEANT upon a coppice gate
  When Frost was spectre-gray,
And Winter's dregs made desolate
    The weakening eye of day.
The tangled bine-stems scored the sky
    Like strings of broken lyres,
And all mankind that haunted nigh
    Had sought their household fires.

The land's sharp features seemed to be
    The Century's corpse outleant,
His crypt the cloudy canopy,
    The wind his death-lament.
The ancient pulse of germ and birth
    Was shrunken hard and dry,
And every spirit upon earth
    Seemed fervourless as I.

At once a voice arose among
    The bleak twigs overhead
In a full-hearted evensong
    Of joy illimited;
An aged thrush, frail, gaunt, and small,
    In blast-beruffled plume,
Had chosen thus to fling his soul
    Upon the growing gloom.

So little cause for carollings
    Of such ecstatic sound
Was written on terrestrial things
    Afar or nigh around,

That I could think there trembled through
　　His happy good-night air
Some blessed Hope, whereof he knew
　　And I was unaware.

December 1900

THE TEMPORARY THE ALL

Sapphics

CHANGE and chancefulness in my flowering
　　youthtime
Set me sun by sun near to one unchosen;
Wrought us fellowlike, and despite divergence,
　　Fused us in friendship.

'Cherish him can I while the true one forthcome
Come the rich fulfiller of my prevision;
Life is roomy yet, and the odds unbounded.'
　　So self-communed I.

Thwart my wistful way did a damsel saunter,
Fair, albeit unformed to be all-eclipsing;
'Maiden meet,' held I, 'till arise my forefelt
　　Wonder of women.'

Long a visioned hermitage deep desiring,
Tenements uncouth I was fain to house in;
'Let such lodging be for a breath-while,' thought I,
　　'Soon a more seemly.

'Then, high handiwork will I make my life-deed,
Truth and Light outshow; but the ripe time pending,
Intermissive aim at the thing sufficeth.'
　　Thus I . . . But lo, me!

28

Mistress, friend, place, aims to be bettered straight-
    way,
Bettered not has Fate or my hand's achievement;
Sole the showance those of my onward earth-track
   Never transcended!

THE GHOST OF THE PAST

WE two kept house, the Past and I,
    The Past and I;
Through all my tasks it hovered nigh,
   Leaving me never alone.
It was a spectral housekeeping
   Where fell no jarring tone,
As strange, as still a housekeeping
   As ever has been known.

As daily I went up the stair
   And down the stair,
I did not mind the Bygone there—
   The Present once to me;
Its moving meek companionship
   I wished might ever be,
There was in that companionship
   Something of ecstasy.

It dwelt with me just as it was,
   Just as it was
When first its prospects gave me pause
   In wayward wanderings,
Before the years had torn old troths
   As they tear all sweet things,

Before gaunt griefs had wrecked old troths
    And dulled old rapturings.

And then its form began to fade,
    Began to fade,
Its gentle echoes faintlier played
    At eves upon my ear
Than when the autumn's look embrowned
    The lonely chambers here,
When autumn's settling shades embrowned
    Nooks that it haunted near.

And so with time my vision less,
    Yea, less and less
Makes of that Past my housemistress,
    It dwindles in my eye;
It looms a far-off skeleton
    And not a comrade nigh,
A flitting fitful skeleton
    Dimming as days draw by.

THE SELF-UNSEEING

HERE is the ancient floor,
    Footworn and hollowed and thin,
Here was the former door
Where the dead feet walked in.

She sat here in her chair,
Smiling into the fire;
He who played stood there,
Bowing it higher and higher.

Childlike, I danced in a dream;
Blessings emblazoned that day;
Everything glowed with a gleam;
Yet we were looking away!

TO LIFE

O LIFE with the sad seared face,
  I weary of seeing thee,
And thy draggled cloak, and thy hobbling pace,
  And thy too-forced pleasantry!

I know what thou would'st tell
  Of Death, Time, Destiny –
I have known it long, and know, too, well
  What it all means for me.

But canst thou not array
  Thyself in rare disguise,
And feign like truth, for one mad day,
  That Earth is Paradise?

I'll tune me to the mood,
  And mumm with thee till eve;
And maybe what as interlude
  I feign, I shall believe!

UNKNOWING

WHEN, soul in soul reflected,
  We breathed an æthered air,
When we neglected
All things elsewhere,

And left the friendly friendless
To keep our love aglow,
  We deemed it endless
  We did not know!

When panting passion-goaded,
We planned to hie away,
  But, unforeboded,
  All the long day
Wild storms so pierced and pattered
That none could up and go,
  Our lives seem shattered . .
  - We did not know!

When I found you, helpless lying,
And you waived my long misprise,
  And swore me, dying,
  In phantom-guise
To wing to me when grieving,
And touch away my woe,
  We kissed, believing
  We did not know!

But though, your powers out-reckoning,
You tarry dead and dumb,
  Or scorn my beckoning,
  And will not come;
And I say, 'Why thus inanely
Brood on her memory so:'
  I say it vainly -
  I feel and know!

HIS FUNERAL

THEY bear him to his resting-place –
In slow procession sweeping by;
I follow at a stranger's space;
His kindred they, his sweetheart I.
Unchanged my gown of garish dye,
Though sable-sad is their attire;
But they stand round with griefless eye,
Whilst my regret consumes like fire!

187-

WS FOR HER MOTHER

I

ONE mile more is
Where your door is
Mother mine! –
Harvest's coming,
Mills are strumming,
Apples fine,
And the cyder made to-year will be as wine.

II

Yet, not viewing
What's a-doing
Here around
Is it thrills me,
And so fills me
That I bound
Like a ball or leaf or lamb along the ground.

f

33

III

Tremble not now
At your lot now
    Silly soul!
Hosts have sped them
Quick to wed them,
    Great and small,
Since the first two sighing half-hearts made a whole.

IV

Yet I wonder,
Will it sunder
    Her from me?
Will she guess that
I said 'Yes,'–that
    His I'd be,
Ere I thought she might not see him as I see!

V

Old brown gable,
Granary, stable,
    Here you are!
O my mother,
Can another
    Ever bar
Mine from thy heart, make thy nearness seem afar?

LOST LOVE

I PLAY my sweet old airs –
The airs he knew
    When our love was true –
    But he does not balk
    His determined walk,
And passes up the stairs.

I sing my songs once more,
   And presently hear
   His footstep near
   As if it would stay;
   But he goes his way,
And shuts a distant door.

So I wait for another morn
   And another night
   In this soul-sick blight;
   And I wonder much
   As I sit, why such
A woman as I was born!

WHERE THE PICNIC WAS

WHERE we made the fire
   In the summer-time
Of branch and briar
On the hill to the sea
I slowly climb
Through winter mire,
And scan and trace
The forsaken place
Quite readily.

Now a cold wind blows,
And the grass is gray,
But the spot still shows
As a burnt circle—aye,
And stick-ends, charred,
Still strew the sward

Whereon I stand,
Last relic of the band
Who came that day!

Yes, I am here
Just as last year,
And the sea breathes brine
From its strange straight line
Up hither, the same
As when we four came.
–But two have wandered far
From this grassy rise
Into urban roar
Where no picnics are,
And one–has shut her eyes
For evermore.

THE GOING

WHY did you give no hint that night
That quickly after the morrow's dawn,
And calmly, as if indifferent quite,
You would close your term here, up and be gone
    Where I could not follow
    With wing of swallow
To gain one glimpse of you ever anon!

    Never to bid good-bye,
    Or lip me the softest call,
Or utter a wish for a word, while I
Saw morning harden upon the wall,
    Unmoved, unknowing
    That your great going
Had place that moment, and altered all.

Why do you make me leave the house
  And think for a breath it is you I see
At the end of the alley of bending boughs
Where so often at dusk you used to be;
    Till in darkening dankness
    The yawning blankness
Of the perspective sickens me!

    You were she who abode
    By those red-veined rocks far West,
You were the swan-necked one who rode
Along the beetling Beeny Crest,
    And, reining nigh me,
    Would muse and eye me,
While Life unrolled us its very best.

Why, then, latterly did we not speak,
Did we not think of those days long dead,
And ere your vanishing strive to seek
That time's renewal? We might have said,
    'In this bright spring weather
    We'll visit together
Those places that once we visited.'

    Well, well! All's past amend,
    Unchangeable. It must go.
I seem but a dead man held on end
To sink down soon. . . . O you could not know
    That such swift fleeing
    No soul foreseeing–
Not even I–would undo me so!

December 1912

'I FOUND HER OUT THERE'

I FOUND her out there
On a slope few see,
That falls westwardly
To the salt-edged air,
Where the ocean breaks
On the purple strand,
And the hurricane shakes
The solid land.

I brought her here,
And have laid her to rest
In a noiseless nest
No sea beats near.
She will never be stirred
In her loamy cell
By the waves long heard
And loved so well.

So she does not sleep
By those haunted heights
The Atlantic smites
And the blind gales sweep,
Whence she would often gaze
At Dundagel's famed head,
While the dipping blaze
Dyed her face fire-red;

And would sigh at the tale
Of sunk Lyonnesse,
As a wind-tugged tress
Flapped her cheek like a flail;

Or listen at whiles
With a thought-bound brow
To the murmuring miles
She is far from now.

Yet her shade, maybe,
Will creep underground
Till it catch the sound
Of that western sea
As it swells and sobs
Where she once domiciled,
And joy in its throbs
With the heart of a child.

December 1912

WITHOUT CEREMONY

IT was your way, my dear,
To be gone without a word
When callers, friends, or kin
Had left, and I hastened in
To rejoin you, as I inferred.

And when you'd a mind to career
Off anywhere—say to town—
You were all on a sudden gone
Before I had thought thereon,
Or noticed your trunks were down.

So, now that you disappear
For ever in that swift style,
Your meaning seems to me
Just as it used to be:
'Good-bye is not worth while!'

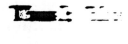
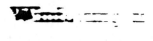

Yes. I have had dreams of that place in the West,
  And a maiden abiding
  Thereat as in hiding;
Fair-eyed and white-shouldered, broad-browed and
  brown-tressed.

And of how, coastward bound on a night long ago,
  There lonely I found her,
  The sea-birds around her,
And other than nigh things uncaring to know.

So sweet her life there (in my thought has it seemed)
  That quickly she drew me
  To take her unto me,
And lodge her long years with me. Such have I
  dreamed.

But nought of that maid from Saint-Juliot I see;
  Can she ever have been here,
  And shed her life's sheen here,
The woman I thought a long housemate with me?

Does there even a place like Saint-Juliot exist?
  Or a Vallency Valley
  With stream and leafed alley,
Or Beeny, or Bos with its flounce flinging mist?

  February 1913

AFTER A JOURNEY

HERETO I come to view a voiceless ghost;
  Whither, O whither will its whim now draw
    me?
Up the cliff, down, till I'm lonely, lost,
  And the unseen waters' ejaculations awe me.

g   41

THE VOICE

WOMAN much missed, how you call to me, call
        to me,
Saying that now you are not as you were
When you had changed from the one who was all to
    me,
But as at first, when our day was fair.

Can it be you that I hear? Let me view you, then,
Standing as when I drew near to the town
Where you would wait for me: yes, as I knew you
    then,
Even to the original air-blue gown!

Or is it only the breeze, in its listlessness
Travelling across the wet mead to me here,
You being ever consigned to existlessness,
Heard no more again far or near?

    Thus I; faltering forward,
    Leaves around me falling,
Wind oozing thin through the thorn from norward
    And the woman calling.

December 1912

A DREAM OR NO

WHY go to Saint-Juliot? What's Juliot to me?
    Some strange necromancy
   But charmed me to fancy
That much of my life claims the spot as its key.

Yes. I have had dreams of that place in the West,
  And a maiden abiding
  Thereat as in hiding;
Fair-eyed and white-shouldered, broad-browed and
    brown-tressed.

And of how, coastward bound on a night long ago,
  There lonely I found her,
  The sea-birds around her,
And other than nigh things uncaring to know.

So sweet her life there (in my thought has it seemed)
  That quickly she drew me
  To take her unto me,
And lodge her long years with me. Such have I
    dreamed.

But nought of that maid from Saint-Juliot I see;
  Can she ever have been here,
  And shed her life's sheen here,
The woman I thought a long housemate with me?

Does there even a place like Saint-Juliot exist?
  Or a Vallency Valley
  With stream and leafed alley,
Or Beeny, or Bos with its flounce flinging mist?

  February 1913

AFTER A JOURNEY

HERETO I come to view a voiceless ghost;
  Whither, O whither will its whim now draw
    me?
Up the cliff, down, till I'm lonely, lost,
  And the unseen waters' ejaculations awe me.

g   41

Where you will next be there's no knowing,
    Facing round about me everywhere,
        With your nut-coloured hair,
And gray eyes, and rose-flush coming and going.

Yes: I have re-entered your olden haunts at last;
    Through the years, through the dead scenes I have
        tracked you;
What have you now found to say of our past—
    Viewed across the dark space wherein I have
        lacked you?
Summer gave us sweets, but autumn wrought divi-
        sion?
    Things were not lastly as firstly well
        With us twain, you tell?
But all's closed now, despite Time's derision.

I see what you are doing: you are leading me on
    To the spots we knew when we haunted here to-
        gether,
The waterfall, above which the mist-bow shone
    At the then fair hour in the then fair weather,
And the cave just under, with a voice still so hollow
    That it seems to call out to me from forty years ago,
        When you were all aglow,
And not the thin ghost that I now frailly follow!

Ignorant of what there is flitting here to see,
    The waked birds preen and the seals flop lazily,
Soon you will have, Dear, to vanish from me,
    For the stars close their shutters and the dawn
        whitens hazily.

Trust me, I mind not, though Life lours,
  The bringing me here; nay, bring me here again!
  I am just the same as when
Our days were a joy, and our paths through flowers.

Pentargan Bay

BEENY CLIFF

March 1870 — March 1913

I

O THE opal and the sapphire of that wandering
      western sea,
And the woman riding high above with bright hair
  flapping free –
The woman whom I loved so, and who loyally loved
  me.

II

The pale mews plained below us, and the waves
  seemed far away
In a nether sky, engrossed in saying their ceaseless
  babbling say,
As we laughed light-heartedly aloft on that clear-
  sunned March day.

III

A little cloud then cloaked us, and there flew an
  irised rain,
And the Atlantic dyed its levels with a dull mis-
  featured stain,
And then the sun burst out again, and purples prinked
  the main.

Still in all its chasmal beauty bulks old Beeny to the
    sky,
And shall she and I not go there once again now
    March is nigh,
And the sweet things said in that March say anew
    there by and by?

V

What if still in chasmal beauty looms that wild weird
    western shore,
The woman now is - elsewhere - whom the ambling
    pony bore,
And nor knows nor cares for Beeny, and will laugh
    there nevermore.

AT CASTLE BOTEREL

AS I drive to the junction of lane and highway,
    And the drizzle bedrenches the waggonette,
I look behind at the fading byway,
    And see on its slope, now glistening wet,
      Distinctly yet

Myself and a girlish form benighted
    In dry March weather. We climb the road
Beside a chaise. We had just alighted
    To ease the sturdy pony's load
      When he sighed and slowed.

What we did as we climbed, and what we talked of
    Matters not much, nor to what it led,
Something that life will not be balked of
    Without rude reason till hope is dead,
      And feeling fled.

44

It filled but a minute. But was there ever
    A time of such quality, since or before,
In that hill's story? To one mind never,
    Though it has been climbed, foot-swift, foot-sore,
        By thousands more.

Primaeval rocks form the road's steep border,
    And much have they faced there, first and last,
Of the transitory in Earth's long order;
    But what they record in colour and cast
        Is - that we two passed.

And to me, though Time's unflinching rigour,
    In mindless rote, has ruled from sight
The substance now, one phantom figure
    Remains on the slope, as when that night
        Saw us alight.

I look and see it there, shrinking, shrinking,
    I look back at it amid the rain
For the very last time; for my sand is sinking,
    And I shall traverse old love's domain
        Never again.

    March 1913

THE PHANTOM HORSEWOMAN

I

QUEER are the ways of a man I know ·
        He comes and stands
        In a careworn craze,
    And looks at the sands
    And the seaward haze

With moveless hands
And face and gaze,
Then turns to go
And what does he see when he gazes so?

II

They say he sees as an instant thing
More clear than to-day,
A sweet soft scene
That once was in play
By that briny green;
Yes, notes alway
Warm, real, and keen,
What his back years bring –
A phantom of his own figuring.

III

Of this vision of his they might say more:
Not only there
Does he see this sight,
But everywhere
In his brain – day, night,
As if on the air
It were drawn rose-bright –
Yea, far from that shore
Does he carry this vision of heretofore:

IV

A ghost-girl-rider. And though, toil-tried,
He withers daily,
Time touches her not,
But she still rides gaily
In his rapt thought

On that shagged and shaly
Atlantic spot,
And as when first eyed
Draws rein and sings to the swing of the tide.

1913

ON A MIDSUMMER EVE

I IDLY cut a parsley stalk
And blew therein towards the moon;
I had not thought what ghosts would walk
With shivering footsteps to my tune.

I went, and knelt, and scooped my hand
As if to drink, into the brook,
And a faint figure seemed to stand
Above me, with the bygone look.

I lipped rough rhymes of chance, not choice,
I thought not what my words might be;
There came into my ear a voice
That turned a tenderer verse for me.

'MY SPIRIT WILL NOT HAUNT THE MOUND'

M Y spirit will not haunt the mound
Above my breast,
But travel, memory-possessed,
To where my tremulous being found
Life largest, best.

My phantom-footed shape will go
　　When nightfall grays
Hither and thither along the ways
I and another used to know
　　In backward days.

And there you'll find me, if a jot
　　You still should care
For me, and for my curious air;
If otherwise, then I shall not,
　　For you, be there.

THE HOUSE OF HOSPITALITIES

HERE we broached the Christmas barrel,
　　Pushed up the charred log-ends;
Here we sang the Christmas carol,
　　And called in friends.

Time has tired me since we met here
　　When the folk now dead were young,
Since the viands were outset here
　　And quaint songs sung.

And the worm has bored the viol
　　That used to lead the tune,
Rust eaten out the dial
　　That struck night's noon.

Now no Christmas brings in neighbours,
　　And the New Year comes unlit;
Where we sang the mole now labours,
　　And spiders knit.

48

Yet at midnight if here walking,
    When the moon sheets wall and tree,
I see forms of old time talking,
    Who smile on me.

'SHUT OUT THAT MOON'

CLOSE up the casement, draw the blind,
    Shut out that stealing moon,
She wears too much the look she wore
    Before our lutes were strewn
With years-deep dust, and names we read
    On a white stone were hewn.

Step not forth on the dew-dashed lawn
    To view the Lady's Chair,
Immense Orion's glittering form,
    The Less and Greater Bear:
Stay in; to such sights we were drawn
    When faded ones were fair.

Brush not the bough for midnight scents
    That come forth lingeringly,
And wake the same sweet sentiments
    They breathed to you and me
When living seemed a laugh, and love
    All it was said to be.

Within the common lamp-lit room
    Prison my eyes and thought;
Let dingy details crudely loom,
    Mechanic speech be wrought:
Too fragrant was Life's early bloom,
    Too tart the fruit it brought!

1904

h

'REGRET NOT ME'

REGRET not me;
  Beneath the sunny tree
I lie uncaring, slumbering peacefully.

  Swift as the light
  I flew my faery flight;
Ecstatically I moved, and feared no night.

  I did not know
  That heydays fade and go,
But deemed that what was would be always so.

  I skipped at morn
  Between the yellowing corn,
Thinking it good and glorious to be born.

  I ran at eves
  Among the piled-up sheaves,
Dreaming, 'I grieve not, therefore nothing grieves.'

  Now soon will come
  The apple, pear, and plum,
And hinds will sing, and autumn insects hum.

  Again you will fare
  To cyder-makings rare,
And junketings; but I shall not be there.

  Yet gaily sing
  Until the pewter ring
Those songs we sang when we went gipsying!

And lightly dance
Some triple-timed romance
In coupled figures, and forget mischance;

And mourn not me
Beneath the yellowing tree;
For I shall mind not, slumbering peacefully.

IN THE MIND'S EYE

THAT was once her casement,
   And the taper nigh,
Shining from within there,
   Beckoned, 'Here am I!'

Now, as then, I see her
   Moving at the pane;
Ah; 'tis but her phantom
   Borne within my brain!~

Foremost in my vision
   Everywhere goes she;
Change dissolves the landscapes,
   She abides with me.

Shape so sweet and shy, Dear,
   Who can say thee nay?
Never once do I, Dear,
   Wish thy ghost away.

AMABEL

I MARKED her ruined hues,
   Her custom-straitened views,
And asked, 'Can there indwell
      My Amabel?'

I looked upon her gown,
Once rose, now earthen brown;
The change was like the knell
        Of Amabel.

Her step's mechanic ways
Had lost the life of May's;
Her laugh, once sweet in swell,
        Spoilt Amabel.

I mused: 'Who sings the strain
I sang ere warmth did wane?
Who thinks its numbers spell
        His Amabel?'-

Knowing that, though Love cease,
Love's race shows no decrease;
All find in dorp or dell
        An Amabel.

-I felt that I could creep
To some housetop and weep
That Time the tyrant fell
        Ruled Amabel!

I said (the while I sighed
That love like ours had died),
'Fond things I'll no more tell
        To Amabel,

'But leave her to her fate,
And fling across the gate,
"Till the Last Trump, farewell,
        O Amabel!"'

1866
16 Westbourne Park Villas

'I SAID TO LOVE'

I SAID to Love,
  'It is not now as in old days
When men adored thee and thy ways
    All else above;
Named thee the Boy, the Bright, the One
Who spread a heaven beneath the sun,'
    I said to Love.

  I said to him,
'We now know more of thee than then;
We were but weak in judgment when,
    With hearts abrim,
We clamoured thee that thou would'st please
Inflict on us thine agonies,'
    I said to him.

  I said to Love,
'Thou art not young, thou art not fair,
No elfin darts, no cherub air,
    Nor swan, nor dove
Are thine; but features pitiless,
And iron daggers of distress,'
    I said to Love.

  'Depart then, Love! . .
  Man's race shall perish, threatenest thou,
Without thy kindling coupling-vow?
The age to come the man of now
    Know nothing of?–

We fear not such a threat from thee;
We are too old in apathy!
Mankind shall cease.—So let it be,'
    I said to Love.

REMINISCENCES OF A DANCING MAN

I

WHO now remembers Almack's balls
    Willis's sometime named
In those two smooth-floored upper halls
    For faded ones so famed?
Where as we trod to trilling sound
The fancied phantoms stood around,
    Or joined us in the maze,
Of the powdered Dears from Georgian years,
Whose dust lay in sightless sealed-up biers,
    The fairest of former days.

II

Who now remembers gay Cremorne,
    And all its jaunty jills,
And those wild whirling figures born
    Of Jullien's grand quadrilles?
With hats on head and morning coats
There footed to his prancing notes
    Our partner-girls and we;
And the gas-jets winked, and the lustres clinked,
And the platform throbbed as with arms enlinked
    We moved to the minstrelsy.

III

Who now recalls those crowded rooms
    Of old yclept 'The Argyle,'

Where to the deep Drum-polka's booms
    We hopped in standard style?
Whither have danced those damsels now!
Is Death the partner who doth moue
    Their wormy chaps and bare?
Do their spectres spin like sparks within
The smoky halls of the Prince of Sin
    To a thunderous Jullien air?

IN A WOOD

PALE beech and pine so blue,
    Set in one clay,
Bough to bough cannot you
    Live out your day?
When the rains skim and skip,
Why mar sweet comradeship,
Blighting with poison-drip
    Neighbourly spray?

Heart-halt and spirit-lame,
    City-opprest,
Unto this wood I came
    As to a nest;
Dreaming that sylvan peace
Offered the harrowed ease—
Nature a soft release
    From men's unrest.

But, having entered in,
    Great growths and small
Show them to men akin—
    Combatants all!

Sycamore shoulders oak,
Bines the slim sapling yoke,
Ivy-spun halters choke
    Elms stout and tall.

Touches from ash, O wych,
    Sting you like scorn!
You, too, brave hollies, twitch
    Sidelong from thorn.
Even the rank poplars bear
Lothly a rival's air,
Cankering in blank despair
    If overborne.

Since, then, no grace I find
    Taught me of trees,
Turn I back to my kind,
    Worthy as these.
There at least smiles abound,
There discourse trills around,
There, now and then, are found
    Life-loyalties.

1887: 1896

HE ABJURES LOVE

AT last I put off love,
    For twice ten years
The daysman of my thought,
    And hope, and doing;
Being ashamed thereof,
    And faint of fears
And desolations, wrought
    In his pursuing,

Since first in youthtime those
    Disquietings
That heart-enslavement brings
    To hale and hoary,
Became my housefellows,
    And, fool and blind,
I turned from kith and kind
    To give him glory.

I was as children be
    Who have no care;
I did not think or sigh,
    I did not sicken;
But lo, Love beckoned me,
    And I was bare,
And poor, and starved, and dry,
    And fever-stricken.

Too many times ablaze
    With fatuous fires,
Enkindled by his wiles
    To new embraces,
Did I, by wilful ways
    And baseless ires,
Return the anxious smiles
    Of friendly faces.

No more will now rate I
    The common rare,
The midnight drizzle dew,
    The gray hour golden,
The wind a yearning cry,
    The faulty fair,

i

Things dreamt, of comelier hue
   Than things beholden! . .

  - I speak as one who plumbs
   Life's dim profound,
One who at length can sound
   Clear views and certain.
But - after love what comes?
   A scene that lours,
A few sad vacant hours,
   And then, the Curtain.
  1883

THE DREAM FOLLOWER

A DREAM of mine flew over the mead
   To the halls where my old Love reigns;
And it drew me on to follow its lead:
  And I stood at her window-panes;

And I saw but a thing of flesh and bone
  Speeding on to its cleft in the clay;
And my dream was scared, and expired on a moan,
  And I whitely hastened away.

WESSEX HEIGHTS

1896

THERE are some heights in Wessex, shaped as
   if by a kindly hand
For thinking, dreaming, dying on, and at crises
   when I stand,

58

Say, on Ingpen Beacon eastward, or on Wylls-Neck
     westwardly,
I seem where I was before my birth, and after death
     may be.

In the lowlands I have no comrade, not even the lone
     man's friend–
Her who suffereth long and is kind; accepts what he
     is too weak to mend:
Down there they are dubious and askance; there
     nobody thinks as I,
But mind-chains do not clank where one's next neigh-
     bour is the sky.

In the towns I am tracked by phantoms having weird
     detective ways–
Shadows of beings who fellowed with myself of earlier
     days:
They hang about at places, and they say harsh heavy
     things
Men with a frigid sneer, and women with tart dis-
     paragings.

Down there I seem to be false to myself, my simple self
     that was,
And is not now, and I see him watching, wondering
     what crass cause
Can have merged him into such a strange continuator
     as this,
Who yet has something in common with himself, my
     chrysalis.

I cannot go to the great gray Plain; there's a figure
     against the moon,

Nobody sees it but I, and it makes my breast beat out
    of tune;
I cannot go to the tall-spired town, being barred by
    the forms now passed
For everybody but me, in whose long vision they
    stand there fast.

There's a ghost at Yell'ham Bottom chiding loud at
    the fall of the night,
There's a ghost in Froom-side Vale, thin-lipped and
    vague, in a shroud of white,
There is one in the railway-train whenever I do not
    want it near,
I see its profile against the pane, saying what I would
    not hear.

As for one rare fair woman, I am now but a thought
    of hers,
I enter her mind and another thought succeeds me
    that she prefers;
Yet my love for her in its fulness she herself even did
    not know;
Well, time cures hearts of tenderness, and now I can
    let her go.

So I am found on Ingpen Beacon, or on Wylls-Neck
    to the west,
Or else on homely Bulbarrow, or little Pilsdon Crest,
Where men have never cared to haunt, nor women
    have walked with me,
And ghosts then keep their distance; and I know
    some liberty.

TO A MOTHERLESS CHILD

AH, child, thou art but half thy darling mother's ·
 Hers couldst thou wholly be,
My light in thee would outglow all in others;
 She would relive to me.
But niggard Nature's trick of birth
 Bars, lest she overjoy,
Renewal of the loved on earth
 Save with alloy.

The Dame has no regard, alas, my maiden,
 For love and loss like mine
No sympathy with mind-sight memory-laden;
 Only with fickle eyne.
To her mechanic artistry
 My dreams are all unknown,
And why I wish that thou couldst be
 But One's alone!

'I NEED NOT GO'

I NEED not go
 Through sleet and snow
To where I know
She waits for me;
She will tarry me there
Till I find it fair,
And have time to spare
From company.

When I've overgot
The world somewhat,

When things cost not
Such stress and strain,
Is soon enough
By cypress sough
To tell my Love
I am come again.

And if some day,
When none cries nay,
I still delay
To seek her side,
(Though ample measure
Of fitting leisure
Await my pleasure)
She will not chide.

What - not upbraid me
That I delayed me,
Nor ask what stayed me
So long? Ah, no! -
New cares may claim me,
New loves inflame me,
She will not blame me,
But suffer it so.

SHELLEY'S SKYLARK

The neighbourhood of Leghorn: March 1887

SOMEWHERE afield here something lies
In Earth's oblivious eyeless trust
That moved a poet to prophecies
A pinch of unseen, unguarded dust:

The dust of the lark that Shelley heard,
And made immortal through times to be;~
Though it only lived like another bird,
And knew not its immortality:

Lived its meek life; then, one day, fell
A little ball of feather and bone;
And how it perished, when piped farewell,
And where it wastes, are alike unknown.

Maybe it rests in the loam I view,
Maybe it throbs in a myrtle's green,
Maybe it sleeps in the coming hue
Of a grape on the slopes of yon inland scene.

Go find it, faeries, go and find
That tiny pinch of priceless dust,
And bring a casket silver-lined,
And framed of gold that gems encrust;

And we will lay it safe therein,
And consecrate it to endless time;
For it inspired a bard to win
Ecstatic heights in thought and rhyme.

WIVES IN THE SERE

I

NEVER a careworn wife but shows,
   If a joy suffuse her,
   Something beautiful to those
      Patient to peruse her,
   Some one charm the world unknows,
      Precious to a muser,

Haply what, ere years were foes,
　　Moved her mate to choose her.

But, be it a hint of rose
　　That an instant hues her,
Or some early light or pose
　　Wherewith thought renews her
Seen by him at full, ere woes
　　Practised to abuse her ~
Sparely comes it, swiftly goes,
　　Time again subdues her.

TO AN UNBORN PAUPER CHILD

I

BREATHE not, hid Heart: cease silently,
And though thy birth-hour beckons thee,
　　Sleep the long sleep:
　　The Doomsters heap
Travails and teens around us here,
And Time-wraiths turn our songsingings to fear.

II

Hark, how the peoples surge and sigh,
And laughters fail, and greetings die:
　　Hopes dwindle; yea,
　　Faiths waste away,
Affections and enthusiasms numb;
Thou canst not mend these things if thou dost come.

III

Had I the ear of wombèd souls
Ere their terrestrial chart unrolls,

And thou wert free
To cease, or be,
Then would I tell thee all I know,
And put it to thee: Wilt thou take Life so?

IV

Vain vow! No hint of mine may hence
To theeward fly: to thy locked sense
Explain none can
Life's pending plan:
Thou wilt thy ignorant entry make
Though skies spout fire and blood and nations quake.

V

Fain would I, dear, find some shut plot
Of earth's wide wold for thee, where not
One tear, one qualm,
Should break the calm.
But I am weak as thou and bare;
No man can change the common lot to rare.

VI

Must come and bide. And such are we
Unreasoning, sanguine, visionary
That I can hope
Health, love, friends, scope
In full for thee; can dream thou'lt find
Joys seldom yet attained by humankind!

THE DEAD MAN WALKING

THEY hail me as one living,
But don't they know
That I have died of late years,
Untombed although?

k   65

I am but a shape that stands here,
    A pulseless mould,
A pale past picture, screening
    Ashes gone cold.

Not at a minute's warning,
    Not in a loud hour,
For me ceased Time's enchantments
    In hall and bower.

There was no tragic transit,
    No catch of breath,
When silent seasons inched me
    On to this death. . . .

    A Troubadour-youth I rambled
        With Life for lyre,
The beats of being raging
    In me like fire.

But when I practised eyeing
    The goal of men,
It iced me, and I perished
    A little then.

When passed my friend, my kinsfolk
    Through the Last Door,
And left me standing bleakly,
    I died yet more;

And when my Love's heart kindled
    In hate of me,
Wherefore I knew not, died I
    One more degree.

And if when I died fully
    I cannot say,
And changed into the corpse-thing
    I am to-day;

Yet is it that, though whiling
    The time somehow
In walking, talking, smiling,
    I live not now.

'I LOOK INTO MY GLASS'

I LOOK into my glass,
    And view my wasting skin,
And say, 'Would God it came to pass
    My heart had shrunk as thin!'

For then, I, undistrest
    By hearts grown cold to me,
Could lonely wait my endless rest
    With equanimity.

But Time, to make me grieve,
    Part steals, lets part abide;
And shakes this fragile frame at eve
    With throbbings of noontide.

EXEUNT OMNES

I

EVERYBODY else, then, going,
    And I still left where the fair was?
Much have I seen of neighbour loungers
    Making a lusty showing,
    Each now past all knowing.

II

There is an air of blankness
In the street and the littered spaces;
Thoroughfare, steeple, bridge and highway
   Wizen themselves to lankness;
   Kennels dribble dankness.

III

Folk all fade. And whither,
As I wait alone where the fair was?
Into the clammy and numbing night-fog
   Whence they entered hither,
   Soon one more goes thither.

June 2, 1913

PART TWO: POEMS NARRATIVE AND REFLECTIVE

PAYING CALLS

I WENT by footpath and by stile
Beyond where bustle ends,
Strayed here a mile and there a mile,
And called upon some friends.

On certain ones I had not seen
For years past did I call,
And then on others who had been
The oldest friends of all.

It was the time of midsummer
When they had used to roam;
But now, though tempting was the air,
I found them all at home.

I spoke to one and other of them
By mound and stone and tree
Of things we had done ere days were dim,
But they spoke not to me.

FRIENDS BEYOND

WILLIAM Dewy, Tranter Reuben, Farmer
Ledlow late at plough,
Robert's kin, and John's, and Ned's,
And the Squire, and Lady Susan, lie in Mellstock
churchyard now!

'Gone,' I call them, gone for good, that group of local
        hearts and heads;
    Yet at mothy curfew-tide,
And at midnight when the noon-heat breathes it back
        from walls and leads

They've a way of whispering to me-fellow-wight
        who yet abide-
    In the muted, measured note
Of a ripple under archways, or a lone cave's stillicide:

'We have triumphed: this achievement turns the
        bane to antidote,
    Unsuccesses to success,
Many thought-worn eves and morrows to a morrow
        free of thought.

'No more need we corn and clothing, feel of old ter-
        restrial stress;
    Chill detraction stirs no sigh;
Fear of death has even bygone us: death gave all
        that we possess.'

W. D.-'Ye mid burn the old bass-viol that I set such
        value by.'
Squire-'You may hold the manse in fee,
    You may wed my spouse, may let my children's
        memory of me die.'

Lady-'You may have my rich brocades, my laces;
        take each household key;
    Ransack coffer, desk, bureau;
Quiz the few poor treasures hid there, con the
        letters kept by me.'

Far.-'Ye mid zell my favourite heifer, ye mid let the
    charlock grow,
  Foul the grinterns, give up thrift.'
Wife-'If ye break my best blue china, children, I
    shan't care or ho.'

All-'We've no wish to hear the tidings, how the
    people's fortunes shift;
  What your daily doings are;
Who are wedded, born, divided; if your lives
    beat slow or swift.

'Curious not the least are we if our intents you
    make or mar,
  If you quire to our old tune,
If the City stage still passes, if the weirs still roar
    afar.'

Thus, with very gods' composure, freed those
    crosses late and soon
  Which, in life, the Trine allow
(Why, none witteth), and ignoring all that haps be-
    neath the moon,

William Dewy, Tranter Reuben, Farmer Ledlow
    late at plough,
  Robert's kin, and John's, and Ned's,
And the Squire, and Lady Susan, murmur mildly to
    me now.

IN FRONT OF THE LANDSCAPE

PLUNGING and labouring on in a tide of visions,
    Dolorous and dear,
Forward I pushed my way as amid waste waters

1

Stretching around,
Through whose eddies there glimmered the cus-
    tomed landscape
    Yonder and near

Blotted to feeble mist. And the coomb and the upland
    Coppice-crowned,
Ancient chalk-pit, milestone, rills in the grass-flat
    Stroked by the light,
Seemed but a ghost-like gauze, and no substantial
    Meadow or mound.

What were the infinite spectacles featuring foremost
    Under my sight,
Hindering me to discern my paced advancement,
    Lengthening to miles;
What were the re-creations killing the daytime
    As by the night?

O they were speechful faces, gazing insistent,
    Some as with smiles,
Some as with slow-born tears that brinily trundled
    Over the wrecked
Cheeks that were fair in their flush-time, ash now
    with anguish,
    Harrowed by wiles.

Yes, I could see them, feel them, hear them, address
    them –
    Halo-bedecked –
And, alas, onwards, shaken by fierce unreason,
    Rigid in hate,
Smitten by years-long wryness born of misprision,
    Dreaded, suspect.

74

Then there would breast me shining sights, sweet
      seasons
   Further in date;
Instruments of strings with the tenderest passion
   Vibrant, beside
Lamps long extinguished, robes, cheeks, eyes with
      the earth's crust
   Now corporate.

Also there rose a headland of hoary aspect
   Gnawed by the tide,
Frilled by the nimb of the morning as two friends
      stood there
   Guilelessly glad
Wherefore they knew not–touched by the fringe of
      an ecstasy
   Scantly descried.

Later images too did the day unfurl me,
   Shadowed and sad,
Clay cadavers of those who had shared in the dramas,
   Laid now at ease,
Passions all spent, chiefest the one of the broad brow
   Sepulture-clad.

So did beset me scenes, miscalled of the bygone,
   Over the leaze,
Past the clump, and down to where'lay the beheld
      ones;
   –Yea, as the rhyme
Sung by the sea-swell, so in their pleading dumbness
   Captured me these.

For, their lost revisiting manifestations
   In their live time

Much had I slighted, caring not for their purport,
  Seeing behind
Things more coveted, reckoned the better worth
    calling
  Sweet, sad, sublime.

Thus do they now show hourly before the intenser
  Stare of the mind
As they were ghosts avenging their slights by my
    bypast
  Body-borne eyes,
Show, too, with fuller translation than rested upon
    them
  As living kind.

Hence wag the tongues of the passing people, saying
  In their surmise,
'Ah~whose is this dull form that perambulates, see-
    ing nought
  Round him that looms
Whithersoever his footsteps turn in his farings,
  Save a few tombs?'

THE CONVERGENCE OF THE TWAIN

Lines on the loss of the 'Titanic'

I

IN a solitude of the sea
  Deep from human vanity,
And the Pride of Life that planned her, stilly couches
    she.

II

Steel chambers, late the pyres
    Of her salamandrine fires,
Cold currents thrid, and turn to rhythmic tidal lyres.

III

Over the mirrors meant
    To glass the opulent
The sea-worm crawls—grotesque, slimed, dumb, in-
    different.

IV

Jewels in joy designed
    To ravish the sensuous mind
Lie lightless, all their sparkles bleared and black and
    blind.

V

Dim moon-eyed fishes near
    Gaze at the gilded gear
And query: 'What does this vaingloriousness down
    here?' . . .

VI

Well: while was fashioning
    This creature of cleaving wing,
The Immanent Will that stirs and urges everything

VII

Prepared a sinister mate
    For her—so gaily great—
A Shape of Ice, for the time far and dissociate.

VIII

And as the smart ship grew
    In stature, grace, and hue,
In shadowy silent distance grew the Iceberg too.

Alien they seemed to be
No mortal eye could see
The intimate welding of their later history,

Or sign that they were bent
By paths coincident
On being anon twin halves of one august event,

Till the Spinner of the Years
Said 'Now!' And each one hears,
And consummation comes, and jars two hemispheres.

THE SCHRECKHORN

With thoughts of Leslie Stephen: June 1897

ALOOF, as if a thing of mood and whim;
Now that its spare and desolate figure gleams
Upon my nearing vision, less it seems
A looming Alp-height than a guise of him
Who scaled its horn with ventured life and limb,
Drawn on by vague imaginings, maybe,
Of semblance to its personality
In its quaint glooms, keen lights, and rugged trim.

At his last change, when Life's dull coils unwind,
Will he, in old love, hitherward escape,
And the eternal essence of his mind
Enter this silent adamantine shape,
And his low voicing haunt its slipping snows
When dawn that calls the climber dyes them rose?

GEORGE MEREDITH

1828-1909

FORTY years back, when much had place
That since has perished out of mind,
I heard that voice and saw that face.

He spoke as one afoot will wind
A morning horn ere men awake;
His note was trenchant, turning kind.

He was of those whose wit can shake
And riddle to the very core
The counterfeits that Time will break.

Of late, when we two met once more,
The luminous countenance and rare
Shone just as forty years before.

So that, when now all tongues declare
His shape unseen by his green hill,
I scarce believe he sits not there.

No matter. Further and further still
Through the world's vaporous vitiate air
His words wing on - as live words will.

May 1909

A SINGER ASLEEP

Algernon Charles Swinburne, 1837-1909

I

IN this fair niche above the unslumbering sea,
That sentrys up and down all night, all day,
From cove to promontory, from ness to bay,

The Fates have fitly bidden that he should be
  Pillowed eternally.

II

-It was as though a garland of red roses
Had fallen about the hood of some smug nun
When irresponsibly dropped as from the sun,
In fulth of numbers freaked with musical closes,
Upon Victoria's formal middle time
  His leaves of rhythm and rhyme.

III

O that far morning of a summer day
When, down a terraced street whose pavements lay
Glassing the sunshine into my bent eyes,
I walked and read with a quick glad surprise
  New words, in classic guise, -

IV

The passionate pages of his earlier years,
Fraught with hot sighs, sad laughters, kisses, tears;
Fresh-fluted notes, yet from a minstrel who
Blew them not naïvely, but as one who knew
  Full well why thus he blew.

V

I still can hear the brabble and the roar
At those thy tunes, O still one, now passed through
That fitful fire of tongues then entered new!
Their power is spent like spindrift on this shore;
  Thine swells yet more and more.

VI

  His singing-mistress verily was no other
Than she the Lesbian, she the music-mother

Of all the tribe that feel in melodies;
Who leapt, love-anguished, from the Leucadian
    steep
Into the rambling world-encircling deep
  Which hides her where none sees.

VII

And one can hold in thought that nightly here
His phantom may draw down to the water's brim,
And hers come up to meet it, as a dim
Lone shine upon the heaving hydrosphere,
And mariners wonder as they traverse near,
  Unknowing of her and him.

VIII

One dreams him sighing to her spectral form:
'O teacher, where lies hid thy burning line;
Where are those songs, O poetess divine
Whose very orts are love incarnadine?'
And her smile back: 'Disciple true and warm,
  Sufficient now are thine.'.

IX

So here, beneath the waking constellations,
Where the waves peal their everlasting strains,
And their dull subterrene reverberations
Shake him when storms make mountains of their
    plains —
Him once their peer in sad improvisations,
And deft as wind to cleave their frothy manes —
I leave him, while the daylight gleam declines
  Upon the capes and chines.

  Bonchurch, 1910

m

IN THE MOONLIGHT

'O LONELY workman, standing there
   In a dream, why do you stare and stare
At her grave, as no other grave there were?

'If your hopeless eyes so importune
Her soul by the shine of this corpse-cold moon,
Maybe you'll raise her phantom soon!'

'Why, fool, it is what I would rather see
Than all the living folk there be;
But alas, there is no such joy for me!'

'Ah-she was one you loved, no doubt,
Through good and evil, through rain and drought,
And when she passed, all your sun went out?'

'Nay: she was the woman I did not love,
Whom all the others were ranked above,
Whom during her life I thought nothing of.'

A CHURCH ROMANCE

Mellstock, circa 1835

SHE turned in the high pew, until her sight
   Swept the west gallery, and caught its row
Of music-men with viol, book, and bow
Against the sinking sad tower-window light.

She turned again; and in her pride's despite
One strenuous viol's inspirer seemed to throw

A message from his string to her below,
Which said: 'I claim thee as my own forthright!'

Thus their hearts' bond began, in due time signed,
And long years thence, when Age had scared
     Romance,
At some old attitude of his or glance
That gallery-scene would break upon her mind,
With him as minstrel, ardent, young, and trim,
Bowing 'New Sabbath' or 'Mount Ephraim.'

THE ROMAN ROAD

THE Roman Road runs straight and bare
  As the pale parting-line in hair
Across the heath. And thoughtful men
Contrast its days of Now and Then,
And delve, and measure, and compare;

Visioning on the vacant air
Helmed legionaries, who proudly rear
The Eagle, as they pace again
                    The Roman Road.

But no tall brass-helmed legionnaire
Haunts it for me. Uprises there
A mother's form upon my ken,
Guiding my infant steps, as when
We walked that ancient thoroughfare,
                    The Roman Road.

THE OXEN

CHRISTMAS Eve, and twelve of the clock.
  'Now they are all on their knees,'
An elder said as we sat in a flock
  By the embers in hearthside ease.

We pictured the meek mild creatures where
  They dwelt in their strawy pen,
Nor did it occur to one of us there
  To doubt they were kneeling then.

So fair a fancy few would weave
  In these years! Yet, I feel,
If some one said on Christmas Eve,
  'Come; see the oxen kneel

'In the lonely barton by yonder coomb
  Our childhood used to know,'
I should go with him in the gloom,
  Hoping it might be so.

SHE HEARS THE STORM

THERE was a time in former years –
  While my roof-tree was his –
When I should have been distressed by fears
  At such a night as this!

I should have murmured anxiously,
  'The pricking rain strikes cold;
His road is bare of hedge or tree,
  And he is getting old.'

But now the fitful chimney-roar,
   The drone of Thorncombe trees,
The Froom in flood upon the moor,
   The mud of Mellstock Leaze,

The candle slanting sooty wick'd,
   The thuds upon the thatch,
The eaves-drops on the window flicked,
   The clacking garden-hatch,

And what they mean to wayfarers,
   I scarcely heed or mind;
He has won that storm-tight roof of hers
   Which Earth grants all her kind.

AFTER THE LAST BREATH

J. H. 1813-1904

THERE'S no more to be done, or feared, or
      hoped;
None now need watch, speak low, and list, and tire;
No irksome crease outsmoothed, no pillow sloped
   Does she require.

Blankly we gaze. We are free to go or stay;
Our morrow's anxious plans have missed their aim;
Whether we leave to-night or wait till day
   Counts as the same.

The lettered vessels of medicaments
Seem asking wherefore we have set them here;
Each palliative its silly face presents
   As useless gear.

And yet we feel that something savours well;
We note a numb relief withheld before;
Our well-beloved is prisoner in the cell
   Of Time no more.

We see by littles now the deft achievement
Whereby she has escaped the Wrongers all,
In view of which our momentary bereavement
   Outshapes but small.

   1904

NIGHT IN THE OLD HOME

WHEN the wasting embers redden the chim-
     ney-breast,
And Life's bare pathway looms like a desert track
   to me,
And from hall and parlour the living have gone to
   their rest,
My perished people who housed them here come
   back to me.

They come and seat them around in their mouldy
   places,
Now and then bending towards me a glance of wist-
   fulness,
A strange upbraiding smile upon all their faces,
And in the bearing of each a passive tristfulness.

'Do you uphold me, lingering and languishing here,
A pale late plant of your once strong stock?'
   I say to them;
'A thinker of crooked thoughts upon Life in the sere,
And on That which consigns men to night after show-
   ing the day to them?'

' O let be the Wherefore! We fevered our years
     not thus:
Take of Life what it grants, without question!' they
     answer me seemingly.
'Enjoy, suffer, wait: spread the table here freely
     like us,
And, satisfied, placid, unfretting, watch Time away
     beamingly!'

THE DEAR

I PLODDED to Fairmile Hill-top, where
     A maiden one fain would guard
From every hazard and every care
     Advanced on the roadside sward.

I wondered how succeeding suns
     Would shape her wayfarings,
And wished some Power might take such ones
     Under its warding wings.

The busy breeze came up the hill
     And smartened her cheek to red,
And hazed her hair. Commiserate still,
     'Good-morning, my Dear!' I said.

She glanced from me to the far-off gray,
     And, with proud severity,
'Good-morning to you – though I may say
     I am not your dear,' quoth she·

'For I am the Dear of one not here –
     One far from his native land!'
And she passed me by; and I did not try
     To make her understand.

1901

87

ONE WE KNEW

M. H. 1772-1857

SHE told how they used to form for the country
 dances—
'The Triumph,' 'The New-rigged Ship'
To the light of the guttering wax in the panelled
 manses,
 And in cots to the blink of a dip.

She spoke of the wild 'poussetting' and 'allemand-
 ing'
 On carpet, on oak, and on sod;
And the two long rows of ladies and gentlemen stand-
 ing,
 And the figures the couples trod.

She showed us the spot where the maypole was yearly
 planted,
 And where the bandsmen stood
While breeched and kerchiefed partners whirled,
 and panted
 To choose each other for good.

She told of that far-back day when they learnt
 astounded
 Of the death of the King of France:
Of the Terror; and then of Bonaparte's unbounded
 Ambition and arrogance.

Of how his threats woke warlike preparations
 Along the southern strand,

And how each night brought tremors and trepida-
    tions
    Lest morning should see him land

She said she had often heard the gibbet creaking
    As it swayed in the lightning flash,
Had caught from the neighbouring town a small
    child's shrieking
    At the cart-tail under the lash

With cap-framed face and long gaze into the embers -
    We seated around her knees
She would dwell on such dead themes, not as one
    who remembers,
    But rather as one who sees.

She seemed one left behind of a band gone distant
    So far that no tongue could hail:
Past things retold were to her as things existent,
    Things present but as a tale.

    May 20, 1902

NEUTRAL TONES

WE stood by a pond that winter day,
    And the sun was white, as though chidden of
       God,
And a few leaves lay on the starving sod,
    - They had fallen from an ash, and were gray.

Your eyes on me were as eyes that rove
Over tedious riddles solved years ago;
And words played between us to and fro
    On which lost the more by our love.

The smile on your mouth was the deadest thing
Alive enough to have strength to die;
And a grin of bitterness swept thereby
    Like an ominous bird a-wing.

Since then, keen lessons that love deceives,
And wrings with wrong, have shaped to me
Your face, and the God-curst sun, and a tree,
    And a pond edged with grayish leaves.

1867
Westbourne Park Villas

TO HIM

PERHAPS, long hence, when I have passed away,
    Some other's feature, accent, thought like mine,
Will carry you back to what I used to say,
And bring some memory of your love's decline.

Then you may pause awhile and think, 'Poor jade!'
And yield a sigh to me - as ample due,
Not as the tittle of a debt unpaid
To one who could resign her all to you -

And thus reflecting, you will never see
That your thin thought, in two small words conveyed,
Was no such fleeting phantom-thought to me,
But the Whole Life wherein my part was played;
And you amid its fitful masquerade
A Thought - as I in yours but seem to be.

1866
Westbourne Park Villas

ROME: THE VATICAN ~ SALA DELLE MUSE

1887

I SAT in the Muses' Hall at the mid of the day,
And it seemed to grow still, and the people to
pass away,
And the chiselled shapes to combine in a haze of sun,
Till beside a Carrara column there gleamed forth
One.

She looked not this nor that of those beings divine,
But each and the whole ~ an essence of all the Nine;
With tentative foot she neared to my halting-place,
A pensive smile on her sweet, small, marvellous face.

'Regarded so long, we render thee sad?' said she.
'Not you,' sighed I, 'but my own inconstancy!
I worship each and each; in the morning one,
And then, alas! another at sink of sun.

'To-day my soul clasps Form; but where is my troth
Of yesternight with Tune: can one cleave to both?'
~'Be not perturbed,' said she. 'Though apart in fame,
As I and my sisters are one, those, too, are the same.'

~'But my love goes further ~ to Story, and Dance, and
Hymn,
The lover of all in a sun-sweep is fool to whim
Is swayed like a river-weed as the ripples run!'
~'Nay, wight, thou sway'st not. These are but phases
of one;

'And that one is I; and I am projected from thee,
One that out of thy brain and heart thou causest to
    be~
Extern to thee nothing. Grieve not, nor thyself becall,
Woo where thou wilt; and rejoice thou canst love at
    all!'

ROME: AT THE PYRAMID OF CESTIUS NEAR THE GRAVES OF SHELLEY AND KEATS

1887

WHO, then, was Cestius,
    And what is he to me?~
Amid thick thoughts and memories multitudinous
    One thought alone brings he.

    I can recall no word
    Of anything he did;
For me he is a man who died and was interred
    To leave a pyramid

    Whose purpose was exprest
    Not with its first design,
Nor till, far down in Time, beside it found their rest
    Two countrymen of mine.

    Cestius in life, maybe,
    Slew, breathed out threatening;
I know not. This I know: in death all silently
    He does a rarer thing,

    In beckoning pilgrim feet
    With marble finger high

To where, by shadowy wall and history-haunted
        street,
    Those matchless singers lie.

    – Say, then, he lived and died
    That stones which bear his name
Should mark, through Time, where two immortal
        Shades abide;
    It is an ample fame.

ON AN INVITATION TO THE UNITED STATES

I

MY ardours for emprize nigh lost
    Since Life has bared its bones to me,
I shrink to seek a modern coast
Whose riper times have yet to be;
Where the new regions claim them free
From that long drip of human tears
Which peoples old in tragedy
Have left upon the centuried years.

II

For, wonning in these ancient lands,
Enchased and lettered as a tomb,
And scored with prints of perished hands,
And chronicled with dates of doom,
Though my own Being bear no bloom
I trace the lives such scenes enshrine,
Give past exemplars present room,
And their experience count as mine.

AT A LUNAR ECLIPSE

THY shadow, Earth, from Pole to Central Sea,
  Now steals along upon the Moon's meek shine
In even monochrome and curving line
Of imperturbable serenity.

How shall I link such sun-cast symmetry
With the torn troubled form I know as thine,
That profile, placid as a brow divine,
With continents of moil and misery?

And can immense Mortality but throw
So small a shade, and Heaven's high human scheme
Be hemmed within the coasts yon arc implies?

Is such the stellar gauge of earthly show,
Nation at war with nation, brains that teem,
Heroes, and women fairer than the skies?

THE SUBALTERNS

I

'POOR wanderer,' said the leaden sky,
    'I fain would lighten thee,
But there are laws in force on high
    Which say it must not be.'

II

~'I would not freeze thee, shorn one,' cried
    The North, 'knew I but how
To warm my breath, to slack my stride;
    But I am ruled as thou.'

III

~ 'To-morrow I attack thee, wight,'
    Said Sickness. 'Yet I swear
I bear thy little ark no spite,
    But am bid enter there.'

IV

'Come hither, Son,' I heard Death say;
    'I did not will a grave
Should end thy pilgrimage to-day,
    But I, too, am a slave!'

V

We smiled upon each other then,
    And life to me had less
Of that fell look it wore ere when
    They owned their passiveness.

THE SLEEP-WORKER

WHEN wilt thou wake, O Mother, wake and
    see ~
As one who, held in trance, has laboured long
By vacant rote and prepossession strong ~
The coils that thou hast wrought unwittingly;

Wherein have place, unrealized by thee,
Fair growths, foul cankers, right enmeshed with
    wrong,
Strange orchestras of victim-shriek and song,
And curious blends of ache and ecstasy? ~

Should that day come, and show thy opened eyes
All that Life's palpitating tissues feel,
How wilt thou bear thyself in thy surprise? ~

Wilt thou déstroy, in one wild shock of shame,
Thy whole high heaving firmamental frame,
Or patiently adjust, amend, and heal?

BEYOND THE LAST LAMP

Near Tooting Common

I

WHILE rain, with eve in partnership,
    Descended darkly, drip, drip, drip,
Beyond the last lone lamp I passed
    Walking slowly, whispering sadly,
    Two linked loiterers, wan, downcast:
Some heavy thought constrained each face,
And blinded them to time and place.

II

The pair seemed lovers, yet absorbed
In mental scenes no longer orbed
By love's young rays. Each countenance
    As it slowly, as it sadly
    Caught the lamplight's yellow glance,
Held in suspense a misery
At things which had been or might be.

III

When I retrod that watery way
Some hours beyond the droop of day,
Still I found pacing there the twain
    Just as slowly, just as sadly,
    Heedless of the night and rain.
One could but wonder who they were
And what wild woe detained them there.

IV

Though thirty years of blur and blot
Have slid since I beheld that spot,
And saw in curious converse there
    Moving slowly, moving sadly
    That mysterious tragic pair,
Its olden look may linger on -
All but the couple; they have gone.

V

Whither? Who knows, indeed. . . . And yet
To me, when nights are weird and wet,
Without those comrades there at tryst
    Creeping slowing, creeping sadly,
    That lone lane does not exist.
There they seem brooding on their pain,
And will, while such a lane remain.

THE FACE AT THE CASEMENT

IF ever joy leave
    An abiding sting of sorrow,
So befell it on the morrow
    Of that May eve. .

    The travelled sun dropped
To the north-west, low and lower,
The pony's trot grew slower,
    Until we stopped.

    ' This cosy house just by
I must call at for a minute,
A sick man lies within it
    Who soon will die.

o

'He wished to marry me,
So I am bound, when I drive near him,
To inquire, if but to cheer him,
     How he may be.'

A message was sent in,
And wordlessly we waited,
Till some one came and stated
     The bulletin.

And that the sufferer said,
For her call no words could thank her;
As his angel he must rank her
     Till life's spark fled.

Slowly we drove away,
When I turned my head, although not
Called to; why I turned I know not
     Even to this day.

And lo, there in my view
Pressed against an upper lattice
Was a white face, gazing at us
     As we withdrew.

And well did I divine
It to be the man's there dying,
Who but lately had been sighing
     For her pledged mine.

Then I deigned a deed of hell;
It was done before I knew it;
What devil made me do it
     I cannot tell!

Yes, while he gazed above,
I put my arm about her
That he might see, nor doubt her
  My plighted Love.

The pale face vanished quick,
As if blasted, from the casement,
And my shame and self-abasement
  Began their prick.

And they prick on, ceaselessly,
For that stab in Love's fierce fashion
Which, unfired by lover's passion,
  Was foreign to me.

She smiled at my caress,
But why came the soft embowment
Of her shoulder at that moment
  She did not guess.

Long long years has he lain
In thy garth, O sad Saint Cleather:
What tears there, bared to weather,
  Will cleanse that stain!

Love is long-suffering, brave,
Sweet, prompt, precious as a jewel;
But O, too, Love is cruel,
  Cruel as the grave.

THE DEAD QUIRE

I

BESIDE the Mead of Memories,
Where Church-way mounts to Moaning Hill,
The sad man sighed his phantasies:
    He seems to sigh them still.

II

' 'Twas the Birth-tide Eve, and the hamleteers
Made merry with ancient Mellstock zest,
But the Mellstock quire of former years
    Had entered into rest.

III

' Old Dewy lay by the gaunt yew tree,
And Reuben and Michael a pace behind,
And Bowman with his family
    By the wall that the ivies bind.

IV

' The singers had followed one by one,
Treble, and tenor, and thorough-bass;
And the worm that wasteth had begun
    To mine their mouldering place.

V

' For two-score years, ere Christ-day light,
Mellstock had throbbed to strains from these;
But now there echoed on the night
    No Christmas harmonies.

VI

'Three meadows off, at a dormered inn,
The youth had gathered in high carouse,
And, ranged on settles, some therein
    Had drunk them to a drowse.

VII

'Loud, lively, reckless, some had grown,
Each dandling on his jigging knee
Eliza, Dolly, Nance, or Joan~
    Livers in levity.

VIII

'The taper flames and hearthfire shine
Grew smoke-hazed to a lurid light,
And songs on subjects not divine
    Were warbled forth that night.

IX

'Yet many were sons and grandsons here
Of those who, on such eves gone by,
At that still hour had throated clear
    Their anthems to the sky.

X

'The clock belled midnight; and ere long
One shouted, "Now 'tis Christmas morn;
Here's to our women old and young,
    And to John Barleycorn!"

XI

'They drink the toast, and shout again:
The pewter-ware rings back the boom,
And for a breath-while follows then
    A silence in the room.

XII

'When nigh without, as in old days,
The ancient quire of voice and string
Seemed singing words of prayer and praise
   As they had used to sing.

XIII

'"While shepherds watch'd their flocks by night,"
Thus swells the long familiar sound
In many a quaint symphonic flight
   To, "Glory shone around."

XIV

'The sons defined their fathers' tones,
The widow his whom she had wed,
And others in the minor moans
   The viols of the dead.

XV

'Something supernal has the sound
As verse by verse the strain proceeds,
And stilly staring on the ground
   Each roysterer holds and heeds.

XVI

'Towards its chorded closing bar
Plaintively, thinly, waned the hymn,
Yet lingered, like the notes afar
   Of banded seraphim.

XVII

'With brows abashed, and reverent tread,
The hearkeners sought the tavern door:
But nothing, save wan moonlight, spread
   The empty highway o'er.

XVIII

'While on their hearing fixed and tense
The aerial music seemed to sink,
As it were gently moving thence
    Along the river brink.

XIX

'Then did the Quick pursue the Dead
By crystal Froom that crinkles there;
And still the viewless quire ahead
    Voiced the old holy air.

XX

'By Bank-walk wicket, brightly bleached,
It passed, and 'twixt the hedges twain,
Dogged by the living; till it reached
    The bottom of Church Lane.

XXI

'There, at the turning, it was heard
Drawing to where the churchyard lay·
But when they followed thitherward
    It smalled, and died away.

XXII

'Each headstone of the quire, each mound,
Confronted them beneath the moon;
But no more floated therearound
    That ancient Birth-night tune.

XXIII

'There Dewy lay by the gaunt yew tree,
There Reuben and Michael, a pace behind,
And Bowman with his family
    By the wall that the ivies bind

XXIV

'As from a dream each sobered son
Awoke, and musing reached his door:
'Twas said that of them all, not one
  Sat in a tavern more.'

XXV

The sad man ceased; and ceased to heed
His listener, and crossed the leaze
From Moaning Hill towards the mead
  The Mead of Memories.

1897

THE PINE PLANTERS

In 'The Woodlanders'

I

FROM the bundle at hand here
  I take each tree,
And set it to stand, here
  Always to be;
When, in a second,
  As if from fear
Of Life unreckoned
  Beginning here,
It starts a sighing
  Through day and night,
Though while there lying
  'Twas voiceless quite.

II

It will sigh in the morning,
  Will sigh at noon,

At the winter's warning,
      In wafts of June;
Grieving that never
      Kind Fate decreed
It should for ever
      Remain a seed,
And shun the welter
      Of things without,
Unneeding shelter
      From storm and drought.

III

Thus, all unknowing
      For whom or what
We set it growing
      In this bleak spot,
It still will grieve here
      Throughout its time,
Unable to leave here,
      Or change its clime;
Or tell the story
      Of us to-day
When, halt and hoary,
      We pass away.

THE BURGHERS

Casterbridge: 17—

THE sun had wheeled from Grey's to Dammer's
      Crest,
And still I mused on that Thing imminent:—
At length I sought the High-street to the West.

The level flare raked pane and pediment,
And my worn face, and shaped my nearing friend
Like one of those the Furnace held unshent.

'I've news concerning her,' he said. 'Attend.
They fly to-night at the late moon's first gleam:
Watch with thy steel: two righteous thrusts will end

Her shameless visions and his passioned dream.
I'll watch with thee, to testify thy wrong –
To aid, maybe. – Law consecrates the scheme.'

I started, and we paced the flags along
Till I replied: 'Since it has come to this
I'll do it! But alone. I can be strong.'

Three hours past Curfew, when the Froom's mild hiss
Reigned sole, undulled by whirr of merchandize,
From Pummery-Tout to where the Gibbet is,

I crossed my pleasaunce hard by Glyd'path Rise,
And stood beneath the wall. Eleven strokes went,
And to the door they came, contrariwise,

And met in clasp so close I had but bent
My lifted blade on either to have let
Their two souls loose upon the firmament.

But something held my arm. 'A moment yet
As pray-time ere you wantons die!' I said;
And then they saw me. Swift her gaze was set

With eye and cry of love illimited
Upon her Heart-king. Never upon me
Had she thrown look of love so thorough-sped!

At once she flung her faint form shieldingly
On his, against the vengeance of my vows;
The which o'erruling, her shape shielded he.

Blanked by such love, I stood as in a drowse,
And the slow moon edged from the upland nigh,
My sad thoughts moving thuswise: 'I may house

And I may husband her, yet what am I
But licensed tyrant to this bonded pair?
Says Charity, Do as ye would be done by.' .

Hurling my iron to the bushes there
I bade them stay. And, as if brain and breast
Were passive, they walked with me to the stair.

Inside the house none watched; and on we prest
Before a mirror, in whose gleam I read
Her beauty, his, – and my own face unblest;

Till at her room I turned. 'Madam,' I said,
'Have you the wherewithal for this? Pray speak.
Love fills no cupboard. You'll need daily bread.'

'We've nothing, sire,' said she; 'and nothing seek.
'Twere base in me to rob my lord unware;
Our hands will earn a pittance week by week.'

And next I saw she had piled her raiment rare
Within the garde-robes, and her household purse,
Her jewels, her least lace of personal wear,

And stood in homespun. Now grown wholly hers,
I handed her the gold, her jewels all,
And him the choicest of her robes diverse.

'I'll take you to the doorway in the wall,
And then adieu,' I told them. 'Friends, withdraw.'
They did so; and she went – beyond recall.

And as I paused beneath the arch I saw
Their moonlit figures – slow, as in surprise
Descend the slope, and vanish on the haw.

'"Fool," some will say,' I thought. 'But who is wise,
Save God alone, to weigh my reasons why?'
– 'Hast thou struck home?' came with the boughs'
  night-sighs.

It was my friend. 'I have struck well. They fly,
But carry wounds that none can cicatrize.'
– 'Not mortal?' said he. 'Lingering – worse,' said I.

THE CORONATION

AT Westminster, hid from the light of day,
Many who once had shone as monarchs lay.

Edward the Pious, and two Edwards more,
The second Richard, Henrys three or four;

That is to say, those who were called the Third,
Fifth, Seventh, and Eighth (the much self-widow-
  ered),

And James the Scot, and near him Charles the Second,
And, too, the second George could there be reckoned.

Of women, Mary and Queen Elizabeth,
And Anne, all silent in a musing death;

108

And William's Mary, and Mary, Queen of Scots,
And consort-queens whose names oblivion blots;

And several more whose chronicle one sees
Adorning ancient royal pedigrees.

–Now, as they drowsed on, freed from Life's old
    thrall,
And heedless, save of things exceptional,

Said one: 'What means this throbbing thudding
    sound
That reaches to us here from overground;

'A sound of chisels, augers, planes, and saws,
Infringing all ecclesiastic laws?

'And these tons-weight of timber on us pressed,
Unfelt here since we entered into rest?

'Surely, at least to us, being corpses royal,
A meet repose is owing by the loyal?'

'–Perhaps a scaffold!' Mary Stuart sighed,
'If such still be. It was that way I died.'

'–Od's! Far more like,' said he the many-wived,
'That for a wedding 'tis this work 's contrived.

'Ha-ha! I never would bow down to Rimmon,
But I had a rare time with those six women!'

'Not all at once?' gasped he who loved confession.
'Nay, nay!' said Hal. 'That would have been trans-
    gression.'

'–They build a catafalque here, black and tall,
Perhaps,' mused Richard, 'for some funeral?'

And Anne chimed in: 'Ah, yes: it may be so!'
'Nay!' squeaked Eliza. 'Little you seem to know–

'Clearly 'tis for some crowning here in state,
As they crowned us at our long bygone date;

'Though we'd no such a power of carpentry,
But let the ancient architecture be;

'If I were up there where the parsons sit,
In one of my gold robes, I'd see to it!'

'But you are not,' Charles chuckled. 'You are here,
And never will know the sun again, my dear!'

'Yea,' whispered those whom no one had addressed;
'With slow, sad march, amid a folk distressed,
We were brought here, to take our dusty rest.

'And here, alas, in darkness laid below,
We'll wait, and listen, and endure the show.
Clamour dogs kingship; afterwards not so!'

1911

A COMMONPLACE DAY

THE day is turning ghost,
    And scuttles from the kalendar in fits and
      furtively,
   To join the anonymous host
Of those that throng oblivion; ceding his place, may-
      be,
   To one of like degree.

I part the fire-gnawed logs,
Rake forth the embers, spoil the busy flames, and lay
    the ends
Upon the shining dogs;
Further and further from the nooks the twilight's
    stride extends,
And beamless black impends.

Nothing of tiniest worth
Have I wrought, pondered, planned; no one thing
    asking blame or praise,
Since the pale corpse-like birth
Of this diurnal unit, bearing blanks in all its rays-
Dullest of dull-hued Days!

Wanly upon the panes
The rain slides, as have slid since morn my colourless
    thoughts; and yet
Here, while Day's presence wanes,
And over him the sepulchre-lid is slowly lowered
    and set,
He wakens my regret.

Regret-though nothing dear
That I wot of, was toward in the wide world at his
    prime,
Or bloomed elsewhere than here,
To die with his decease, and leave a memory sweet,
    sublime,
Or mark him out in Time. .

-Yet, maybe, in some soul,
In some spot undiscerned on sea or land, some impulse
    rose,

Or some intent upstole
Of that enkindling ardency from whose maturer glows
    The world's amendment flows;

    But which, benumbed at birth
By momentary chance or wile, has missed its hope to
        be
Embodied on the earth;
And undervoicings of this loss to man's futurity
    May wake regret in me.

HER DEATH AND AFTER

THE summons was urgent, and forth I went
    By the way of the Western Wall, so drear
On that winter night, and sought a gate —
    Where one, by Fate,
    Lay dying that I held dear.

And there, as I paused by her tenement,
And the trees shed on me their rime and hoar,
I thought of the man who had left her lone —
    Him who made her his own
    When I loved her, long before.

The rooms within had the piteous shine
That home-things wear when there's aught amiss;
From the stairway floated the rise and fall
    Of an infant's call,
    Whose birth had brought her to this.

Her life was the price she would pay for that whine—
For a child by the man she did not love.

'But let that rest for ever,' I said,
    And bent my tread
  To the bedchamber above.

She took my hand in her thin white own,
And smiled her thanks-though nigh too weak
And made them a sign to leave us there,
    Then faltered, ere
  She could bring herself to speak.

'Just to see you before I go-he'll condone
Such a natural thing now my time's not much
When Death is so near it hustles hence
    All passioned sense
  Between woman and man as such!

'My husband is absent. As heretofore
The City detains him. But, in truth,
He has not been kind. . . . I will speak no blame,
    But-the child is lame;
  O, I pray she may reach his ruth!

'Forgive past days-I can say no more-
Maybe if we'd wedded you'd now repine!
But I treated you ill. I was punished. Farewell!
    Truth shall I tell?
  Would the child were yours and mine!

'As a wife I've been true. But, such my unease
That, could I insert a deed back in Time,
I'd make her yours, to secure your care;
    And the scandal bear,
  And the penalty for the crime!'

~When I had left, and the swinging trees
Rang above me, as lauding her candid say,
Another was I. Her words were enough:
    Came smooth, came rough,
  I felt I could live my day.

Next night she died; and her obsequies
In the Field of Tombs where the earthworks frowned
Had her husband's heed. His tendance spent,
    I often went
  And pondered by her mound.

All that year and the next year whiled,
And I still went thitherward in the gloam;
But the Town forgot her and her nook,
    And her husband took
  Another Love to his home.

And the rumour flew that the lame lone child
Whom she wished for its safety child of mine,
Was treated ill when offspring came
    Of the new-made dame,
  And marked a more vigorous line.

A smarter grief within me wrought
Than even at loss of her so dear,
That the being whose soul my soul suffused
    Had a child ill-used,
  I helpless to interfere!

One eve as I stood at my spot of thought
In the white-stoned Garth with these brooding
    glooms,

114

Her husband neared; and to shun his nod
    By her hallowed sod
  I went from among the tombs

To the Cirque of the Gladiators which faced
That haggard mark of Imperial Rome,
Whose Pagan echoes mock the chime
    Of our Christian time
  From its hollows of turf and loam.

The sun's gold touch was just displaced
From the vast Arena where men once bled,
When her husband followed; bowed; half-passed,
    With lip upcast;
  Then, halting, sullenly said:

'It is noised that you visit my first wife's tomb.
Now, I gave her an honoured name to bear
While living, when dead. So I've claim to ask
    Your right to task
  My patience by darkling there?

'There's decency even in death, I assume;
Preserve it, sir, and keep away;
For the mother of my first-born you
    Show mind undue!
  - Sir, I've nothing more to say.'

A desperate stroke discerned I then-
God pardon-or pardon not-the lie;
She had sighed that she wished (lest the child should
    pine
    Of slights) 'twere mine,
  So I said: 'But the father I.

'That you thought it yours is the way of men;
But I won her troth long ere your day·
You learnt how, in dying, she summoned me?
        'Twas in fealty.
    ~Sir, I've nothing more to say,

'Save that, if you'll hand me my little maid,
I'll take her, and rear her, and spare you toil.
Think it more than a friendly act none can;
        I'm a lonely man,
    While you've a large pot to boil.

'If not, and you'll put it to ball or blade
To-night, to-morrow night, anywhen~
I'll meet you here. . . . But think of it,
        And in season fit
    Let me hear from you again.

    Well, I went away, hoping; but nought I heard
Of my stroke for the child, till there greeted me
A little voice that one day came
        To my window-frame
    And babbled innocently:

'My father, who's not my own, sends word
I'm to stay here, sir, where I belong!'
Next a writing came: 'Since the child was the fruit
        Of your lawless suit,
    Pray take her, to right a wrong.'

And I did. And I gave the child my love,
And the child loved me, and estranged us none.
But compunctions loomed; for I'd harmed the dead
        By what I'd said
    For the good of the living one.

116

– Yet though, God wot, I am sinner enough,
And unworthy the woman who drew me so,
Perhaps this wrong for her darling's good
        She forgives, or would,
    If only she could know!

IN DEATH DIVIDED

I

I SHALL rot here, with those whom in their day
        You never knew,
    And alien ones who, ere they chilled to clay,
        Met not my view,
Will in your distant grave-place ever neighbour you.

II

    No shade of pinnacle or tree or tower,
        While earth endures,
    Will fall on my mound and within the hour
        Steal on to yours;
One robin never haunt our two green covertures.

III

    Some organ may resound on Sunday noons
        By where you lie,
    Some other thrill the panes with other tunes
        Where moulder I;
No selfsame chords compose our common lullaby.

IV

    The simply-cut memorial at my head
        Perhaps may take

A rustic form, and that above your bed
　　A stately make;
No linking symbol show thereon for our tale's sake.

V

And in the monotonous moils of strained, hard-run
　　Humanity,
　The eternal tie which binds us twain in one
　　No eye will see
Stretching across the miles that sever you from me.

IN TENEBRIS

　　Considerabam ad dexteram, et videbam: et non erat qui
cognosceret me.... Non est qui requirat animam meam.'–Ps. cxli.

WHEN the clouds' swoln bosoms echo back the
　　　shouts of the many and strong
That things are all as they best may be, save a few to
　　be right ere long,
And my eyes have not the vision in them to discern
　　what to these is so clear,
The blot seems straightway in me alone; one better
　　he were not here.

The stout upstanders chime, All's well with us: ruers
　　have nought to rue!
　　　what the potent so often say, can it fail to be
　　somewhat true?
Breezily go they, breezily come; their dust smokes
　　around their career,
　　I think I am one born out of due time, who has no
　　calling here.

Their dawns bring lusty joys, it seems; their even-
   ings all that is sweet;
Our times are blessed times, they cry: Life shapes
   it as is most meet,
And nothing is much the matter; there are many
   smiles to a tear;
Then what is the matter is I, I say. Why should such
   an one be here? . . .

Let him in whose ears the low-voiced Best is killed
   by the clash of the First,
Who holds that if way to the Better there be, it exacts
   a full look at the Worst,
Who feels that delight is a delicate growth cramped
   by crookedness, custom, and fear,
Get him up and be gone as one shaped awry; he dis-
   turbs the order here.

1895-96

'I HAVE LIVED WITH SHADES'

I

I HAVE lived with Shades so long,
   So long have talked to them,
Since from the forest's hem
I sped to street and throng,·
      That sometimes they
      In their dim style
      Will pause awhile
      To hear my say;

II

And take me by the hand,
And lead me through their rooms

In the To-be, where Dooms
Half-wove and shapeless stand:
   And show from there
   The dwindled dust
   And rot and rust
   Of things that were.

III

'Now turn,' they said to me
One day: 'Look whence we came,
And signify his name
Who gazes thence at thee.'–
   –'Nor name nor race
   Know I, or can,'
   I said, 'Of man
   So commonplace.

IV

'He moves me not at all;
I note no ray or jot
Of rareness in his lot,
Or star exceptional.
   Into the dim
   Dead throngs around
   He'll sink, nor sound
   Be left of him.'

V

'Yet,' said they, 'his frail speech,
Hath accents pitched like thine–
Thy mould and his define
A likeness each to each–

But go! Deep pain
Alas, would be
His name to thee,
And told in vain!'

Feb. 2, 1899

A POET

ATTENTIVE eyes, fantastic heed,
Assessing minds, he does not need,
Nor urgent writs to sup or dine,
Nor pledges in the rosy wine.

For loud acclaim he does not care
By the august or rich or fair,
Nor for smart pilgrims from afar,
Curious on where his hauntings are.

But soon or later, when you hear
That he has doffed this wrinkled gear,
Some evening, at the first star-ray,
Come to his graveside, pause, and say:

'Whatever his message – glad or grim –
Two bright-souled women clave to him';
Stand and say that while day decays,
It will be word enough of praise.

July 1914

PART THREE: WAR POEMS AND LYRICS FROM THE DYNASTS

EMBARKATION

Southampton Docks

HERE, where Vespasian's legions struck the
     sands,
And Cerdic with his Saxons entered in,
And Henry's army leapt afloat to win
Convincing triumphs over neighbour lands,

Vaster battalions press for further strands,
To argue in the self-same bloody mode
Which this late age of thought, and pact, and code,
Still fails to mend. ~ Now deckward tramp the bands,

Yellow as autumn leaves, alive as spring;
And as each host draws out upon the sea
Beyond which lies the tragical To-be,
None dubious of the cause, none murmuring,

Wives, sisters, parents, wave white hands and smile,
As if they knew not that they weep the while.

DEPARTURE

Southampton Docks

WHILE the far farewell music thins and fails,
    And the broad bottoms rip the bearing brine
All smalling slowly to the gray sea line ~
And each significant red smoke-shaft pales,

Keen sense of severance everywhere prevails,
Which shapes the late long tramp of mounting men
To seeming words that ask and ask again:
'How long, O ruling Teutons, Slavs, and Gaels

'Must your wroth reasonings trade on lives like these,
That are as puppets in a playing hand?—
When shall the saner softer polities
Whereof we dream, have sway in each proud land,
And patriotism, grown Godlike, scorn to stand
Bondslave to realms, but circle earth and seas?'

THE GOING OF THE BATTERY

I

RAIN came down drenchingly; but we unblench-
　　ingly
Trudged on beside them through mirk and through
　　mire,
They stepping steadily—only too readily!—
Scarce as if stepping brought parting-time nigher.

II

Great guns were gleaming there, living things seem-
　　ing there,
Cloaked in their tar-cloths, upmouthed to the night;
Wheels wet and yellow from axle to felloe,
Throats blank of sound, but prophetic to sight.

III

Gas-glimmers drearily, blearily, eerily
Lit our pale faces outstretched for one kiss,
While we stood prest to them, with a last quest to them
Not to court perils that honour could miss.

IV

Sharp were those sighs of ours, blinded these eyes
　　of ours,
When at last moved away under the arch

126

All we loved. Aid for them each woman prayed for
    them,
Treading back slowly the track of their march.

V

Someone said: 'Nevermore will they come: ever-
    more
Are they now lost to us.' O it was wrong!
Though may be hard their ways, some Hand will
    guard their ways,
Bear them through safely, in brief time or long.

VI

--Yet, voices haunting us, daunting us, taunting us,
Hint in the night-time when life beats are low
Other and graver things ... Hold we to braver things,
Wait we, in trust, what Time's fulness shall show.

DRUMMER HODGE

I

THEY throw in Drummer Hodge, to rest
    Uncoffined--just as found:
His landmark is a kopje-crest
    That breaks the veldt around;
And foreign constellations west
    Each night above his mound.

II

Young Hodge the Drummer never knew--
    Fresh from his Wessex home

The meaning of the broad Karoo,
The Bush, the dusty loam,
And why uprose to nightly view
Strange stars amid the gloam.

III

Yet portion of that unknown plain
Will Hodge for ever be;
His homely Northern breast and brain
Grow up a Southern tree,
And strange-eyed constellations reign
His stars eternally.

THE MAN HE KILLED

'HAD he and I but met
By some old ancient inn,
We should have sat us down to wet
Right many a nipperkin!

'But ranged as infantry,
And staring face to face,
I shot at him as he at me,
And killed him in his place.

'I shot him dead because —
Because he was my foe,
Just so: my foe of course he was;
That's clear enough; although

'He thought he'd 'list, perhaps,
Off-hand like — just as I —
Was out of work — had sold his traps
No other reason why.

'Yes; quaint and curious war is!
    You shoot a fellow down
You'd treat if met where any bar is,
    Or help to half-a-crown.'
1902

THE SOULS OF THE SLAIN

I

THE thick lids of Night closed upon me
    Alone at the Bill
    Of the Isle by the Race¹ -
Many-caverned, bald, wrinkled of face
And with darkness and silence the spirit was on me
    To brood and be still.

II

No wind fanned the flats of the ocean,
    Or promontory sides,
    Or the ooze by the strand,
Or the bent-bearded slope of the land,
Whose base took its rest amid everlong motion
    Of criss-crossing tides.

III

Soon from out of the Southward seemed nearing
    A whirr, as of wings
    Waved by mighty-vanned flies,
Or by night-moths of measureless size,
And in softness and smoothness well-nigh beyond
        hearing
    Of corporal things.

¹ The 'Race' is the turbulent sea-area off the Bill of Portland,
where contrary tides meet.

IV

And they bore to the bluff, and alighted
  A dim-discerned train
  Of sprites without mould,
Frameless souls none might touch or might hold
On the ledge by the turreted lantern, far-sighted
  By men of the main.

V

And I heard them say 'Home!' and I knew them
  For souls of the felled
  On the earth's nether bord
Under Capricorn, whither they'd warred,
And I neared in my awe, and gave heedfulness to
    them
  With breathings inheld.

VI

Then, it seemed, there approached from the north-
    ward
  A senior soul-flame
  Of the like filmy hue:
And he met them and spake: 'Is it you,
O my men?' Said they, 'Aye! We bear homeward
    and hearthward
  To feast on our fame!'

VII

'I've flown there before you,' he said then:
  'Your households are well;
  But–your kin linger less
On your glory and war-mightiness

Than on dearer things.'–'Dearer?' cried these from
    the dead then,
      'Of what do they tell?'

VIII

'Some mothers muse sadly, and murmur
    Your doings as boys –
    Recall the quaint ways
Of your babyhood's innocent days.
Some pray that, ere dying, your faith had grown
    firmer,
      And higher your joys.

IX

'A father broods: "Would I had set him
    To some humble trade,
    And so slacked his high fire,
And his passionate martial desire;
Had told him no stories to woo him and whet him
    To this dire crusade!"'

X

'And, General, how hold out our sweethearts,
    Sworn loyal as doves?'
    'Many mourn; many think
It is not unattractive to prink
Them in sables for heroes. Some fickle and fleet
    hearts
      Have found them new loves.'

XI

'And our wives?' quoth another resignedly,
    'Dwell they on our deeds?'

~'Deeds of home; that live yet
Fresh as new~deeds of fondness or fret;
Ancient words that were kindly expressed or un-
    kindly,
These, these have their heeds.'

XII

'Alas! then it seems that our glory
    Weighs less in their thought
    Than our old homely acts,
And the long-ago commonplace facts
Of our lives~held by us as scarce part of our story,
    And rated as nought!'

XIII

Then bitterly some: 'Was it wise now
    To raise the tomb-door
    For such knowledge? Away!'
But the rest: 'Fame we prized till to-day;
Yet that hearts keep us green for old kindness we
    prize now
    A thousand times more!'

XIV

Thus speaking, the trooped apparitions
    Began to disband
    And resolve them in two:
Those whose record was lovely and true
Bore to northward for home: those of bitter traditions
    Again left the land,

XV

And, towering to seaward in legions,
    They paused at a spot

Overbending the Race –
That engulphing, ghast, sinister place
Whither headlong they plunged, to the fathomless
        regions
    Of myriads forgot.

XVI

And the spirits of those who were homing
    Passed on, rushingly,
    Like the Pentecost Wind;
And the whirr of their wayfaring thinned
And surceased on the sky, and but left in the gloaming
    Sea-mutterings and me.

December, 1899

'MEN WHO MARCH AWAY'

Song of the Soldiers

WHAT of the faith and fire within us
    Men who march away
    Ere the barn-cocks say
    Night is growing gray,
Leaving all that here can win us;
What of the faith and fire within us
    Men who march away?

Is it a purblind prank, O think you,
    Friend with the musing eye,
    Who watch us stepping by
    With doubt and dolorous sigh?
Can much pondering so hoodwink you!
Is it a purblind prank, O think you,
    Friend with the musing eye?

Nay. We well see what we are doing,
  Though some may not see –
  Dalliers as they be –
  England's need are we;
Her distress would leave us rueing:
Nay. We well see what we are doing,
  Though some may not see!

In our heart of hearts believing
  Victory crowns the just,
  And that braggarts must
  Surely bite the dust,
Press we to the field ungrieving,
In our heart of hearts believing
  Victory crowns the just.

Hence the faith and fire within us
  Men who march away
  Ere the barn-cocks say
  Night is growing gray,
Leaving all that here can win us;
Hence the faith and fire within us
  Men who march away.

September 5, 1914

BEFORE MARCHING, AND AFTER

In Memoriam F. W. G.

ORION swung southward aslant
  Where the starved Egdon pine-trees had
    thinned,
  The Pleiads aloft seemed to pant
  With the heather that twitched in the wind;
But he looked on indifferent to sights such as these,

Unswayed by love, friendship, home joy or home
    sorrow,
And wondered to what he would march on the
    morrow.

    The crazed household clock with its whirr
    Rang midnight within as he stood,
    He heard the low sighing of her
    Who had striven from his birth for his good;
But he still only asked the spring starlight, the breeze,
What great thing or small thing his history would
    borrow
From that Game with Death he would play on the
    morrow.

    When the heath wore the robe of late summer,
    And the fuchsia-bells, hot in the sun,
    Hung red by the door, a quick comer
    Brought tidings that marching was done
For him who had joined in that game overseas
Where Death stood to win; though his memory would
    borrow
A brightness therefrom not to die on the morrow.

    September, 1915

IN TIME OF 'THE BREAKING OF NATIONS'

I

ONLY a man harrowing clods
    In a slow silent walk
    With an old horse that stumbles and nods
    Half asleep as they stalk.

II

Only thin smoke without flame
　　From the heaps of couch grass:
Yet this will go onward the same
　　Though Dynasties pass.

III

Yonder a maid and her wight
　　Come whispering by;
War's annals will cloud into night
　　Ere their story die.

FROM 'THE DYNASTS'

THE NIGHT OF TRAFALGAR

Boatman's Song

I

IN the wild October night-time, when the wind
raved round the land,
And the Back-sea met the Front-sea, and our doors
were blocked with sand,
And we heard the drub of Dead-man's Bay, where
bones of thousands are,
We knew not what the day had done for us at
Trafalgar.
Had done,
Had done,
For us at Trafalgar!

II

'Pull hard, and make the Nothe, or down we go!' one
says, says he.
We pulled; and bedtime brought the storm; but
snug at home slept we.
Yet all the while our gallants after fighting through
the day,
Were beating up and down the dark, sou'-west of
Cadiz Bay.
The dark,
The dark,
Sou'-west of Cadiz Bay!

The victors and the vanquished then the storm it
 tossed and tore,
As hard they strove, those worn-out men, upon that
 surly shore;
Dead Nelson and his half-dead crew, his foes from
 near and far,
Were rolled together on the deep that night at
 Trafalgar.
The deep,
The deep,
That night at Trafalgar!

HUSSAR'S SONG: 'BUDMOUTH DEARS'

I

WHEN we lay where Budmouth Beach is,
 O the girls were fresh as peaches
With their tall and tossing figures and their eyes of
 blue and brown!
 And our hearts would ache with longing
 As we paced from our sing-songing
With a smart 'Clink! Clink!' up the Esplanade
 and down.

II

 They distracted and delayed us
 By the pleasant pranks they played us,
And what marvel, then, if troopers, even of regiments
 of renown,
 On whom flashed those eyes divine, O,

Should forget the countersign, O,
As we tore 'Clink! Clink!' back to camp above the
  town.

III

Do they miss us much, I wonder,
Now that war has swept us sunder,
And we roam from where the faces smile to where
  the faces frown?
And no more behold the features
Of the fair fantastic creatures,
And no more 'Clink! Clink!' past the parlours of
  the town?

IV

Shall we once again there meet them?
Falter fond attempts to greet them?
Will the gay sling-jacket glow again beside the muslin
  gown? –
Will they archly quiz and con us
With a sideway glance upon us,
While our spurs 'Clink! Clink!' up the Esplanade
  and down?

'MY LOVE'S GONE A-FIGHTING'

Country-girl's Song

I

MY Love's gone a-fighting
  Where war-trumpets call,
The wrongs o' men righting
  Wi' carbine and ball,
And sabre for smiting,
  And charger, and all!

II

Of whom does he think there
  Where war-trumpets call,
To whom does he drink there,
  Wi' carbine and ball
On battle's red brink there,
  And charger, and all?

III

Her, whose voice he hears humming
  Where war-trumpets call,
'I wait, Love, thy coming
  Wi' carbine and ball,
And bandsmen a-drumming
  Thee, charger and all!'

THE EVE OF WATERLOO

Chorus of Phantoms

THE eyelids of eve fall together at last,
  And the forms so foreign to plain and tree
Lie down as though native, and slumber fast.

Sore are the thrills of misgiving we see
In the artless green growths at this harlequinade,
Distracting a vigil where calm should be!

The sod seems opprest, and the field afraid
Of a Something to come, whereof these are the
    proofs,–
Neither earthquake, nor storm, nor eclipse's shade.

Yea, the coneys are scared by the thud of hoofs,
And their white scuts flash at their vanishing heels,
And swallows abandon the hamlet-roofs.

The mole's tunnelled chambers are crushed by
    wheels,
The lark's eggs scattered, their owners fled,
And the hare's hid litter the sapper unseals.

The snail draws in at the terrible tread,
But in vain; he is crushed by the felloe-rim;
The worm asks what can be overhead,

And wriggles deep from a scene so grim,
And guesses him safe; for he does not know
What a foul red rain will be soaking him.

Beaten about by the heel and toe
Are butterflies, sick of the day's long rheum,
To die of a worse than the weather-foe.

Trodden and bruised to a miry tomb
Are ears that have greened but will never be gold,
And flowers in the bud that will never bloom.

So the season's intent, ere its fruit unfold,
Is frustrate, and mangled, and made succumb,
Like a youth of promise struck stark and cold.

And what of these who to-night have come?
– The young sleep sound; but the weather awakes
In the veterans, pains from the past that numb;

Old stabs of Ind, old Peninsular aches,
Old Friedland chills, haunt their moist mud bed;
Cramps from Austerlitz; till their slumber breaks.

And each soul sighs as he shifts his head
On the loam he's to lease with the other dead
From to-morrow's dew-fall till Time be sped.

CHORUS OF THE PITIES

After the Battle

SEMICHORUS I

TO Thee whose eye all nature owns,
  Who hurlest Dynasts from their thrones,[1]
And liftest those of low estate
We sing, with Her men consecrate!

II

Yea, Great and Good, Thee, Thee we hail,
Who shak'st the strong, Who shield'st the frail,
Who hadst not shaped such souls as we
If tender mercy lacked in Thee!

I

Though times be when the mortal moan
Seems unascending to Thy throne,
Though seers do not as yet explain
Why Suffering sobs to Thee in vain;

II

We hold that Thy unscanted scope
Affords a food for final Hope,
That mild-eyed Prescience ponders nigh
Life's loom, to lull it by and by.

I

Therefore we quire to highest height
The Wellwiller, the kindly Might
That balances the Vast for weal,
That purges as by wounds to heal.

[1] καθεῖλε ΔΥΝΑΣΤΑΣ ἀπὸ θρόνων.—Magnificat.

The systemed suns the skies enscroll
Obey Thee in their rhythmic roll,
Ride radiantly at Thy command,
Are darkened by Thy Masterhand!

I

And these pale panting multitudes
Seen surging here, their moils, their moods,
All shall 'fulfil their joy' in Thee,
In Thee abide eternally!

II

Exultant adoration give
The Alone, through Whom all living live,
The Alone, in Whom all dying die,
Whose means the End shall justify! Amen.

LAST CHORUS

SEMICHORUS I OF THE YEARS

LAST as first the question rings
Of the Will's long travailings;
Why the All-mover,
Why the All-prover
Ever urges on and measures out the droning tune of
Things.[1]

II

Heaving dumbly
As we deem,
Moulding numbly
As in dream,
Apprehending not how fare the sentient subjects of
Its scheme.

[1] Hor. Epis. i. 12

SEMICHORUS I OF THE PITIES

Nay;-shall not Its blindness break?
Yea, must not Its heart awake,
        Promptly tending
        To Its mending
In a genial germing purpose, and for loving-kindness'
    sake?

II

        Should It never
        Curb or cure
        Aught whatever
        Those endure
Whom It quickens, let them darkle to extinction swift
    and sure.

CHORUS

        But-a stirring thrills the air
        Like to sounds of joyance there
            That the rages
            Of the ages
Shall be cancelled, and deliverance offered from the
    darts that were,
Consciousness the Will informing, till It fashion all
    things fair!

HERE END THE SELECTED POEMS OF
THOMAS HARDY, O.M., NOW PRINTED IN
THE RICCARDI PRESS FOUNT AT THE
CHISWICK PRESS BY ARRANGEMENT
WITH MESSRS. MACMILLAN & CO. LTD.
PUBLISHED BY PHILIP LEE WARNER
FOR THE MEDICI SOCIETY, LTD.
AT VII GRAFTON ST., LONDON
& AT DCCLV BOYLSTON
STREET, BOSTON
MCMXXI

CPSIA information can be obtained at www.ICGtesting.com
Printed in the USA
LVOW07s1028190616

493234LV00042B/668/P